WHAT IS GOING ON IN
CHRISTIAN CRISIS PREGNANCY
COUNSELLING?

WHAT IS GOING ON IN
CHRISTIAN CRISIS PREGNANCY
COUNSELLING?

DR E. S. WILLIAMS

THE WAKEMAN TRUST, LONDON
& BELMONT HOUSE PUBLISHING

What is Going On in Christian Crisis Pregnancy Counselling?
© Dr E. S. Williams, 2005

THE WAKEMAN TRUST & BELMONT HOUSE PUBLISHING
(Wakeman Trust is a UK Registered Charity)

Wakeman Trust
UK Registered Office
38 Walcot Square
London SE11 4TZ

Wakeman US Office
300 Artino Drive
Oberlin, OH 44074-1263
Website: www.wakemantrust.org

Belmont House Publishing
36 The Crescent
Belmont
Sutton SM2 6BJ
Website: www.belmonthouse.co.uk

ISBN 1 870855 45 0

Cover design by Andrew Owen
Cover photograph: Steve Allen, Science Photo Library (unborn child, 12 weeks)

Printed by Stephens & George, Merthyr Tydfil, UK

Contents

Foreword
by Dr Peter Masters

WHEN SO VERY MANY expectant mothers are seeking abortion advice, and when we hear the staggering news that one-in-ten Lambeth girls become pregnant when aged fifteen to seventeen, we are glad to know that numerous Christian counselling centres have been established. Such efforts surely merit our strong, prayerful support. But something deeply disturbing has come to pass in these centres, over time, as this troubling book shows.

Dr Ted Williams, a medical doctor of long experience, and a noted specialist in the public health field, shows how the leading Christian counselling agency has adopted a deeply compromised approach which is ready to provide 'non-judgemental' advice that leaves in place the option of abortion. By embracing in essence the non-judgemental, options counselling of secular humanism, distinctive Christian values are seriously undermined.

Expectant mothers, including so many girls, should be helped in a spirit of great compassion, but they must always be advised according to the Book of God, and its eternal values. These are tragic days, when the distinctive standards of the Lord are increasingly being set aside. This book will not only inform and warn, but it will also serve to focus the aims of pastors and all other Christians as they extend help to expectant mothers who seek it.

Dr Williams has interacted personally with the leading figures of compromised counselling, but their methods are now so well-established that Christians everywhere have a right to know what is going on.

Significantly this alarm is being issued at the same time as a book by my wife entitled, *Building an Outreach Sunday School*. This is a plea to evangelical churches to re-establish and enlarge Sunday Schools so that the rising generation may learn moral values and the message of the Gospel, matters which will be unknown to millions of children, unless Sunday Schools are revived.

May Dr Williams' book also serve – albeit indirectly – as an alarm call to Christians to take up once again the work of vigorous children's outreach, the best and most positive response to unfettered promiscuity, the gravest and saddest problem of our age.

PETER MASTERS

Metropolitan Tabernacle
June, 2005

1
Crisis Pregnancy Counselling

MASS ABORTION is one of the greatest moral evils in Great Britain. In the four decades since the Abortion Act received royal assent in October 1967 there have been over six million legal abortions, the number currently running at about 180 thousand per year. This means that on an average weekday around 700 legal abortions are performed in National Health Service (NHS) hospitals and private abortion clinics around the country. Such is the cold, calculating approach of the British Government that it has a national standard to increase to fifty percent the percentage of NHS funded abortions undertaken before ten weeks gestation. To help achieve this target the Department of Health has allocated special funds to improve access to abortion services. What is so disturbing about the situation is that, with the exception of a few pro-life organisations, there is hardly any opposition to mass abortion.

The last century saw a sea change in British attitudes to abortion. In the nineteenth century there was a Christian consensus that abortion was wrong. It was widely believed that biblical truth taught that human life is unique, for each person is created in the image of God. All human life, therefore, should be protected and loved. The Christian view sought to incorporate its belief in the sanctity of human life into the British legal framework. Accordingly the Offences Against the Person Act of 1861 made it a criminal offence to procure an abortion in any circumstances. The unborn child had the full protection of the law.

By the 1960s the heart of the Christian church had grown cold and compromise was the order of the day. Abortion was no longer regarded as a sin against Heaven and against the unborn child, but a pragmatic solution to a social problem. The relative morality of situation ethics claimed that abortion, under certain circumstances, was the only 'loving' pragmatic solution to an unwanted pregnancy. The abortion lobby was skilled in manipulating language to hide the reality of their campaign – the unborn child became a 'foetus' and abortion was referred to as a 'termination'. The changing sexual mores of the permissive society demanded the right for women to choose whether they wanted a pregnancy to continue or not. At last the ideas of the radicals, liberals, humanists, feminists and socialists, for so long contained by the restraints of biblical truth, had become the new consensus with a new relative morality. 'Free love' and 'pro-choice' were the slogans of the sexual revolutionaries.

Abortion Act of 1967

During the permissive 1960s there had been four unsuccessful attempts to legalise abortion when in 1966 David Steel, a young Liberal MP, came third in the ballot for a Private Member's Bill and agreed to sponsor the Abortion Reform Bill. Behind David Steel was the Abortion Law Reform Association which had been set up in the 1930s by a group of socialist feminists. A number of prominent figures in the Labour Party were supporters of abortion reform, including the Minister of Health, Kenneth Robinson, who had put his own Private Member's Bill to Parliament in the early 1960s. Roy Jenkins, the Home Secretary, expressed his support for reforming what he called the existing harsh and archaic law on abortion. Labour's tacit support in allowing extra parliamentary time was essential to the success of the Bill.

The Abortion Act of 1967 was a watershed in the revolt against traditional morality. It represented a massive victory for the dark forces of the sexual revolution. It was the ultimate rejection of all that was good and decent, a rejection of compassion and honesty. The dagger of pro-choice, which allowed women to choose to abort their unborn child, was plunged into the heart of civilised Britain. The most vulnerable in society were now subject to attack from the abortionist's curette. A once great Christian nation had chosen to sacrifice its unborn children on the altar of pro-choice.

One of the most devastating consequences of the abortion holocaust has been its effect on the national birth rate. Few people understand that since 1972, just a few years after the Abortion Act came into force, the fertility rate in Britain has declined steadily and is now 25 per cent below that required to replace the population by natural means. The result is fewer children and young people in society – 180,000 fewer each year. The national decline in fertility is perhaps the most important social trend of our lifetime. The consequences for schools, universities and the economy are obvious. It is one of the reasons why so many doctors and nurses are being imported to run the NHS. This is one of the main reasons why there is a looming pensions crisis, which will become even more acute as the number of economically active people in the population declines. The terrible consequences of the Abortion Act are slowly being worked out in our society.

CARE's stand on abortion

One of the leading Christian organisations standing against abortion is CARE (Christian Action, Research and Education), a well-established mainstream Christian charity. It believes that Christians, through God's strength, can change society for the better. Through parliamentary campaigning, CARE is seeking to influence public policy on key moral issues, including abortion. It seeks to use prayer and spiritual strength as it stands in the vanguard of defending Christian values not only in the UK but worldwide.[1] Its mission 'is to declare Christian truth and demonstrate Christ's compassion in society'.[2] It believes that its strength 'lies in the combined use of caring, campaigning and intercessory prayer and its commitment to the practical application of biblical truth'.[3] CARE has established a network of crisis pregnancy counselling centres to help individual Christians and local churches make a positive impact on their communities and on the nation at large. It has also set up CARE*confidential*, an on-line counselling service for women with unplanned pregnancies.

All, however, is not what it seems, because the counselling methods employed by CARE have drifted far away from the values of their mission statement as we shall in due course show.

CARE's Chairman, Lyndon Bowring, in his 'Dear Friend' newsletter (November 2004), asks whether a woman's 'right' to choose abortion is to be protected – even at the expense of denying that most precious gift from God, life, to the child in her womb? 'It has been one *[of]* our strongest passions from CARE's earliest days, to defend the dignity and sanctity of human life itself. We believe that we have a responsibility as Christians to be a voice for the voiceless, because they are defenceless, and because God alone gave them life. Our 162 Centres, committed to helping women facing pregnancy crises, continually seek to offer understanding and support – and at the same time underlining our belief that all human beings are made in the image of God, and are of supreme value.'[4]

Reading this impassioned plea one is left with the clear impression that CARE, as 'a voice for the voiceless', is a pro-life organisation that is opposed to abortion. This is the message that is being presented to those who support CARE as a bastion that stands against the evil of abortion. But how many of those who read this newsletter are aware of the nature of the advice that CARE Centres give to pregnant women? The purpose of this book is to examine CARE's crisis pregnancy counselling programme in the light of biblical truth.

CARE's Network of Pregnancy Counselling Centres

CARE has a network of pregnancy counselling centres scattered around the UK. CARE Centres Network is an organisation that is concerned about the welfare of women in relation to pregnancy, including abortion. The first pregnancy counselling centre opened in Basingstoke in 1986, followed by another in Southampton in 1987. As further centres opened around the country, a need grew for an umbrella organisation to support them, to develop resources and to train counsellors. The website of CARE Centres Network (www.care.org.uk/ccn) advertises the fact that its centres provide information for women with an unplanned pregnancy and their partners. The centres provide a free pregnancy test, confidential counselling and post-abortion counselling. Women with a positive test are promised that a trained advisor will 'listen to you, give you all the information you need, help you find out what you want to do'.[5] CARE's 2003 annual report makes the further point that 'to combat the increase in pregnancy testing and abortion referral clinics, many centres are including preventative work in their support of young people'.[6]

In addition to its counselling centres CARE has a national freephone helpline, CAREconfidential, which offers confidential counselling to anyone facing pregnancy or post-abortion problems – whatever their age, beliefs, background or circumstances. It provides concerned women with free nationwide access to trained advisors, 'accurate information on all the options and sensitive, confidential counselling to help you reach your own informed choice'.[7] It also provides 'links to local agencies for further support, whatever decision is made'.[8]

The Head of CARE Centres Network, Joanna Thompson, in her keynote message at the Network's annual conference, attended by nearly 400 delegates, said the climate was starting to change at both local and national level. 'God is starting to bring us more and more into the public arena. We're going to become even more visible. With the ongoing development of our schools work and "evaluate" – CARE's new sex and relationships education programme – I think more schools will welcome us. Workers are engaging with their communities more and more.' She reflected on the Network's beginnings 20 years ago. 'God has built something that we couldn't have imagined then – 160 centres, a national helpline, a network of trained volunteers, schools work – the list goes on!'[9]

Pro-choice counselling

A number of secular pro-choice organisations offer pregnancy counselling from a stance that accepts that women have a right to abortion.

The British Pregnancy Advisory Service (BPAS), established in 1968, is the country's largest abortion provider. It aims to provide a safe, legal abortion service. BPAS supports what it calls 'reproductive choice' by providing services to prevent or end unwanted pregnancy with contraception or by abortion. It offers pregnancy testing, crisis pregnancy counselling, abortion services up to 24 weeks of pregnancy, after-abortion support and emergency contraception. A BPAS leaflet, *Unplanned pregnancy: your choices*, is an example of the pro-choice approach to pregnancy counselling. The leaflet explains that it 'is not intended to encourage you to make any particular decision. Instead it offers ideas that have been helpful to other women in making the decision that was right for them.'

However, BPAS has recently received adverse publicity for apparently ignoring the British law on abortion by referring women for late abortion (after 24 weeks gestation) to an abortion clinic in Spain. As a result of the furore surrounding its actions, BPAS went on the offensive by calling on the Government to change the law limiting late abortion. BPAS chief executive, Ann Furedi, said: 'Abortion is safe, it's legal, and it's our job to make it acceptable and easy for women.'[10]

A number of other secular agencies have websites that provide on-line pro-choice counselling. Marie Stopes International UK claims to be the country's leading reproductive healthcare charity. With nine specialist centres and a network of GP partners the organisation offers expert help and advice to women with an unplanned pregnancy. Marie Stopes recognises that 'the decision to continue with a pregnancy is one of the biggest and most life-changing decisions a woman will ever make. This is why we believe that all women should have the right to choose for themselves. If a woman decides that an abortion is in her or her family's best interests, for whatever reason or reasons, she should have access to safe, supportive and non-judgemental advice and help. No one should pressure her into either continuing with the pregnancy or having an abortion.' The on-line counselling guide helps a woman decide what she should do about her pregnancy. 'We hope that this interactive guide, which has been developed by a Marie Stopes International counsellor, will help you decide what to do.'[11] The website of the Irish Family Planning Association (IFPA) provides information for pregnant women: 'If you know you are pregnant it is important that you discuss your *choices* with someone straight away.'[12]

The Oxford University Student Union (OUSU) is an organisation that has taken a strong pro-choice position. It believes 'that every woman should have the right to choose'. The Union feels so strongly on this point that it has passed a resolution to condemn directive advice groups, and to instigate a ban on any such group. The Union continues to provide students with information on unplanned pregnancy and non directional advice.[13]

A large number of American organisations are in the forefront of pro-choice counselling, such as Planned Parenthood, Pro-choice Connection and the National Abortion Federation. In the next chapter we examine the approach of pro-choice organisations and compare it with the messages offered by CARE's crisis pregnancy counselling service.

Endnotes

1 CARE, *Dear Friend Newsletter*, February 2005.
2 CARE, *With CARE*, leaflet.
3 Ibid.

4 CARE, *Dear Friend Newsletter*, November 2004, Right to choose?

5 CARE Centres Network website, It's positive – what are my options?

6 CARE, 2003 annual report, pp 4-5.

7 CARE*confidential* website, for pregnancy & post-abortion help.

8 Ibid.

9 *Care* Today, Spring 2005, Issue 8, Half-time for game of life, pp 6-7.

10 National Right to Life, newsletter, December 2004, British doctors send women to Spain for late abortions, Liz Townsend.

11 Marie Stopes International UK website, On-line counselling guide, How do you feel about your pregnancy?

12 Irish Family Planning Association website, Pregnancy counselling, how can you be sure you are pregnant?

13 Oxford University Student Union website, main/campaigns/promoting choice/OUSU policy towards abortion.

2

Pro-Choice Messages

TO UNDERSTAND the messages of pro-choice abortion counselling I have examined information from various prominent British pro-choice organisations, as well as a number of American organisations such as Planned Parenthood Federation of America, National Abortion Federation and Pro-choice Connection. Primary sources of pro-choice counselling are the leaflets, *Unplanned pregnancy: your choices* (BPAS) and *Unsure about your pregnancy? A guide to making the right decision for you* (National Abortion Federation), and the websites of the Irish Family Planning Association (IFPA) and Marie Stopes International.

Four sources have been used to describe CARE's approach to abortion counselling – the leaflet *Making a Decision*, the CARE Centres Network website, the CAREconfidential website and the manual for Christian pregnancy crisis counselling, *Called to Care*.

Below is the result of my examination of the various counselling approaches. By including numerous quotations, I have endeavoured to let the organisations speak for themselves. Various phrases are italicised to identify common themes. Information from pro-choice organisations is presented first, followed by CARE.

Objective of pregnancy counselling

The objective of pro-choice counselling is to help a woman to find out what she really wants to do about her unplanned pregnancy. **BPAS** encourages a woman to consider a number of factors so that she can make the best decision for herself at the time: 'But what you can do is carefully consider your plans, your values, and your feelings, and then make *the best decision for you at the time*.'[1] **Planned Parenthood** helps a woman to answer the question: 'How can I decide *which choice is best for me*?'[2] **Pro-choice Connection** explains that it is important for a woman to know what she really wants to do about her pregnancy: 'It's getting to know what those feelings actually mean that will help you have a fuller understanding of *what you really want to do*.'[3] The **National Abortion Federation** booklet explains to a woman who is having second thoughts about her pregnancy: 'If that is no longer *what you want*, or if you didn't intend to get pregnant in the first place, you can start looking more closely at how you feel about being pregnant.'[4]

According to the **CARE Centres Network** website the objective of counselling is to help a woman discover what she wants to do with her pregnancy. The website explains that 'a pregnancy counselling centre is a place where you can spend as much time as you want to talk with a trained advisor confidentially. She will listen to you, give you all the information you need, help you find out *what you want to do*.'[5]

Offering a pregnant woman options

The starting point of pro-choice counselling is to provide a woman with a number of options from which she can choose what she wants to do about her pregnancy. The BPAS, Planned Parenthood, Pro-choice Connection, National Abortion Federation and the IFPA all offer a woman the same three options.

BPAS: 'If you are pregnant you have *three basic choices*; continue the pregnancy, place the baby for adoption, end the pregnancy now by having an abortion.'[6] According to BPAS: 'If you cannot decide, you may *need to get more information about your choices*.'[7]

Planned Parenthood: 'You have *three choices* if you are pregnant. You can choose to have a baby and raise the child, you can choose to have a baby and place the child for adoption, you can choose to end the pregnancy.'[8] Planned Parenthood states that 'a pro-choice organisation will tell the caller they provide full and accurate *information on all options* including abortion.'[9]

IFPA: Clients are told that within the counselling session, '*full information on all your options* is available. Whether continuing your pregnancy and parenting, considering adoption or abortion, the counsellor will take you through the practical aspects *of each choice* and provide helpful information.'[10]

National Abortion Federation: 'If you are pregnant, you have *three basic choices*.'[11]

Pro-choice Connection: 'There are *three possibilities* to consider: terminating the pregnancy; putting the baby up for adoption; and becoming a mother . . .'[12]

CARE's pregnancy counselling service provides a woman with the same three options. The leaflet *Making a Decision* advises, 'When you're ready, you and your husband or partner will need to consider the *options available*: parenting, adoption or abortion.'[13] The leaflet continues, 'with *each of the options open to you*, there are gains and losses involved . . . write a list of those things you think you might lose with each of the options.'[14] **CARE Centres Network** in response to the question, 'What are my options?' informs a woman: '*You have three options*: continue with the pregnancy, adoption, abortion. You are entitled to have all the information about all three options.'[15] **CARE-confidential** provides 'accurate information on all the options'.[16]

Non-directive counselling

Pro-choice counselling stresses that its counselling is impartial, non-directive, and non-judgemental. As mentioned above, the pro-choice Oxford University Student Union feels so strongly on this point that it has a policy to condemn any groups that give directive advice; it has instigated an advertising ban on any such groups. In pro-choice counselling all three options are given equal weight and a woman is not advised that any one particular option is better or worse than any other. The counsellor does not mind what a woman chooses, so long as she makes her own decision.

'**BPAS** provides accurate information about abortion and *non-judgemental counselling.*'[17] The **Family Planning Association** 'believes that all women who want it should have access to free *non-directive pregnancy counselling* and post-abortion counselling'.[18] The **IFPA** website states that: 'Organisations like the IFPA offer *non-directive counselling.* This means that the counsellor has no opinion on what is best for you.'[19] **Planned Parenthood** informs its clients: 'A pro-choice organisation will tell the caller that they are pro-choice, that they offer unbiased, *non-judgemental counselling* on all unplanned pregnancy options including parenting, adoption and abortion.'[20] **Brook Advisory Centres** says that it 'sees many young people every year with unplanned pregnancies and we believe that it is vital that those young people receive *impartial, non-judgemental counselling.*'[21] **Marie Stopes** declares: 'A consultation for unplanned pregnancy at Marie Stopes Reproductive Choices includes . . . *non-judgemental and non-directive counselling.*'[22] The **National Abortion Federation** leaflet says: 'If an agency tells you that abortion is unsafe or immoral, that is a clue that they are not interested in helping you make your own decision; call the National Abortion Federation's hotline for the name of an agency that will give you accurate information and *non-judgemental* assistance.'[23]

CARE also stresses that its counselling approach is impartial, non-judgemental and non-directive. The **CARE Centres Network** website explains to a pregnant woman: 'Trained advisors are trained in *non-directional counselling,* enabling you to discover more clearly how you feel about the situation you are in.'[24] The leaflet, *More about*

CARE*confidential*, reassures a woman, 'All our trained advisors are required to adhere to the ethos of CARE*confidential*, which is to provide caring support and *impartial information . . .*'[25] The Hull Crisis Pregnancy Centre, part of CARE's network, explains: 'We are here to help people work through pregnancy-related issues in a *non-judgemental way.*'[26]

Advice based on experience

Pro-choice counselling is guided by the subjective experience of the counsellors, and not any objective standard of right and wrong. The **BPAS** leaflet states that the 'ideas in this leaflet are *based on our experience* of talking about unplanned pregnancy with almost 50,000 women every year.'[27] The **IFPA** makes the same point: 'The ideas below are *based on our experience* of talking about unplanned pregnancy with hundreds of women every year.'[28] Similarly, **Pro-choice Connection**: 'An *experienced* options counsellor can help you think things through.'[29] **National Abortion Federation**: 'The ideas in this booklet are based on our experience counselling thousands of women.'[30]

CARE counsellors provide a pregnant woman with a list of questions to help her decide what to do that are '*based on our experience* of helping those who have had abortions'.[31]

Examining feelings

Pro-choice counselling believes that a woman's feelings should play an important part in the decision-making process. The BPAS leaflet, *Unplanned pregnancy: your choices* uses the word 'feel/feelings' twenty times. National Abortion Federation's leaflet, *Unsure about your pregnancy? A guide to making the right decision for you*, mentions 'feel/feelings' twenty times. Marie Stopes' on-line counselling guide uses 'feelings' or 'feel/felt' twenty-two times. Pro-choice Connection website mentions the words thirty-two times. Below are some examples:

BPAS leaflet: 'To show *how you are feeling* at the moment, try to finish each of these sentences. The idea of *having a baby makes me feel . . .*'

'You might *feel concerned* about how other people may react.'

'You might *feel worried* about being unable to cope.'

'An unintended pregnancy can arouse many *different feelings*. Most women find they have mixed or *conflicting feelings*.'

'How do you *feel about being pregnant*? The idea of having an *abortion makes me feel . . .*'

Marie Stopes on-line counselling guide: 'We hope this interactive guide . . . will help you analyse *your feelings*.'

'When you discovered you were pregnant, what were your *initial feelings*?'

'How do you *feel now*?'

'Do you *feel OK about having a child* on your own?'

'Do you *feel your* family and friends will support you?'

'Do you *feel you can cope* with this pregnancy and having a child on your own?'

'How do you *feel about having an abortion*?'

Pro-choice Connection on-line guide: 'It's important to *talk about your feelings*.'

'*Identifying your feelings*, and understanding what they mean to you, will help you in your decision-making process.'

'As you think about your pregnancy, *how do you feel*? Give yourself all the space you need to fully realise *your feelings*.'

National Abortion Federation leaflet: 'We hope you will use these ideas to help you become clear about your own thoughts and *feelings*.'

'How do you *feel* about being pregnant?'

'You might *feel worried* about being able to manage a baby.'

'List the *different feelings* you have right now about being pregnant.'

'The idea of having an abortion makes me *feel . . .*'

'Since you probably have *conflicting feelings* about each choice, you may find that whatever decision you make won't *feel* like the "perfect" decision. It is natural to continue to have some *mixed feelings*. Ask yourself, "Can I handle those *feelings*?"'

CARE also invites a woman to consult her feelings to help her make a decision. A striking observation is that the CARE Centres Network website uses the words 'feel' or 'feelings' twenty-four times and the leaflet *Making a Decision* twenty-three times. The manual *Called to Care* advises the counsellor in the event of a positive pregnancy test to ask the woman, 'What are you feeling about it?' Below are some statements that illustrate the importance CARE counselling places on subjective emotions:

CARE Centres Network website: 'Pregnancy counselling centres are there to help you find out how *you feel* about having an abortion.'

'Many *feel* that they just couldn't cope. Difficult circumstances *feel overwhelming.*'

'When faced with an unplanned pregnancy, many *women feel* as if one part of them is telling them one thing and a different part another. How far are you *feeling this split?*'

'What do you *feel you would gain* by having an abortion?'

CARE's leaflet, *Making a Decision*: 'You may be *feeling shocked and numb* at the moment.'

'Ask yourself what *your instinctive feelings* are about each option.'

'Having looked at all the facts and explored thoroughly how *you feel about each option*, you may be ready to make your decision.'

Clarifying personal values

Pro-choice counselling invites a woman to focus on her personal values, on her own beliefs, to the exclusion of any objective moral standard outside of herself.

BPAS: 'Now that you have explored your choices, and *clarified your feelings and values* about the choices, you may be ready to make a decision.'[32]

IFPA: 'Professional, confidential and supportive counselling can *help you clarify your personal situation and feelings.*'[33]

CARE asks a woman to consider her personal values. 'This is to do

with the *things you believe* are right or wrong – *your personal values* . . .
Draw a circle on paper to represent *your circle of values*. Put a dot in the
middle to *represent you*. Think about abortion, parenthood and adoption separately . . . where are they in relation to *your circle of values*?
Inside, outside, somewhere else? Put a cross on the diagram where *you
feel they go*.' [34]

Informed choice

The idea of 'informed choice' is central to abortion counselling. Pro-
choice counselling invites a woman to make an 'informed choice'
between the three options, based on the information she has received
and guided by her feelings. **BPAS** states that its 'current policy is one of
adapting to each individual by the provision of information, the provision of support, clarifying that every woman understands all options
open to her. This will enable a woman to be respected in her decision
and make an *informed choice*.'[35] **Planned Parenthood** tells its clients
that its counsellors 'will provide information to help women and cou-
ples make *informed choices*'.[36] **Brook Advisory Centres** believe that 'it is
every woman's right to have access to impartial information about
abortion, as well as support in making *an informed decision* about pregnancy.' 'Brook believes that young people should be helped to make
informed decisions that are right for them in the long term.'[37] A **Marie
Stopes** booklet on abortion has been designed to help a woman 'reach
an informed decision' about the options available to her.[38] The Sexwise
project, which consists of a website and radio programmes, has been
developed jointly by the **International Planned Parenthood Federation**
and the BBC World Service, to speak to people in different regions of
the world about sexual health and reproductive rights, which include
the right to abortion. A key aim of Sexwise is to assist people to make
more *informed choices* about their sexuality.[39]

A leading aim of **CARE's** counselling process is to guide a woman to
a position where she is able to make her own informed decision.
According to *Called to CARE* one of the main goals of counselling is to

bring a woman 'to the point where she can make a *fully informed deci-sion*'.[40] CARE advisors are trained to give 'accurate information about all the options open to you so that you can make *an informed choice*'.[41] **CARE Centres Network** advises a woman: 'You are entitled to this information so that you and your partner can make *an informed choice*.'[42] **CARE*confidential*** provides 'confidential counselling to help you reach your *own informed choice*'.[43]

The final decision

Pro-choice counselling encourages a woman to make a decision that she can live with, based on what she feels to be the right choice for her at the time. The decision must be her own, and she must resist any outside influences that might try to persuade her to follow a particular view. The **BPAS** leaflet explains to a woman, 'Because you probably have conflicting feelings about each choice, you may find that whatever decision you make won't feel like the perfect decision. Ask yourself, "*Can I live with those feelings?*"'[44] **Planned Parenthood** advises, 'There is no right or wrong choice for everyone. Only *you can decide which choice is right for you*.'[45] So a woman must ask herself: 'Which *choice(s) could I live with?*'[46] According to **Pro-choice Connection**: 'Whatever your decision is, it is important that *you feel it is your own*.'[47]

CARE advises a woman to make a decision that she can live with, on the basis of the facts about each option and her feelings. **CARE's** *Making a Decision* explains: 'Make sure you have read all the factual information about each option before you make a final decision. Having looked at all the facts and explored thoroughly how you feel about each option, you may be ready to make your decision. It's important that *you feel able to live with* the decision you have made.'[48] **CARE Centres Network** advises: 'It is important for you to have all the information so that *you can decide for yourself*.'[49] And more: 'You cannot go back in time; you can only go forward – and now you must make *the decision that you can live with*.'[50] ***Called to Care*** puts it this way: 'She has received all the important information necessary and discussed all her options in depth. She understands more clearly the consequences of each option but now has to decide which set of consequences she is going to give priority. She has to make *the decision she can live with*.'[51]

The relative morality of pro-choice dogma

To understand pro-choice counselling we must understand that it operates in a world of relative morality that rejects absolute standards of right and wrong. Most people in the pro-abortion camp believe that a woman's right to abortion should not be restricted by moral considerations. Dr Joseph Fletcher, Professor of Ethics at the Episcopal Theological Seminary, and the father of situation ethics, explained the essence of the new morality in a lecture in 1965: 'It all depends on the situation. In certain circumstances unmarried love could be infinitely more normal than married love. Lying could be more Christian than telling the truth. Stealing could be better than respecting private property.'[52] As far as sexual conduct is concerned, Fletcher makes it plain in *Situation Ethics* (1966) that no behaviour is right or wrong in itself. The prostitute who by the services she provides helps a man to shed his sexual inhibitions is to be commended for her contribution to the 'love ethic'. According to Fletcher, 'Whether any form of sex (hetero, homo, or auto) is good or evil depends on whether love is fully served.'[53]

Fletcher's approach to abortion was entirely pragmatic. Decisions are not made on the basis of absolute moral laws, but on the basis of a rational calculation of the probable consequences: '. . . there are in the end only two ways of deciding what is right. Either we will obey a rule (or a ruler) of conscience, which is the *a priori* or prejudiced approach, or we will look as reasonably as we can at the facts and calculate the consequences, the human costs and benefits – the pragmatic way . . . Most of us decide for or against things on the principle of proportionate good. We try to figure out the gains and losses that would follow from one course of action or another and then choose the one that is best, the one that offers the most good. This calculation of consequences is often called a trade-off or cost-benefit analysis.'[54] This is the moral framework of pro-choice counselling. In the eyes of the pro-abortionist there is no absolute moral obligation on a mother to protect the life of her unborn child. On the contrary, the baby is simply one item in a cost-benefit analysis.

According to this way of thinking abortion is not wrong and there are circumstances in which it is seen to be the only sensible, practical option. Pro-choice counselling is content to work within a relative moral framework that depends on circumstances and feelings. So it presents a menu of options from which a woman can make her prag-matic choice. As there is no moral distinction between keeping the pregnancy and aborting the baby, the best choice depends on what the woman feels she can live with.

Behind the moral relativism of pro-choice lies the godless philosophy of existentialism, which has slowly evolved during the second half of the 20th century into the ideology of postmodernism. Since everyone creates his or her own 'truth', every 'truth' is equally valid. Since every-one does what is right in their own eyes, all moral choices are of equal worth. It follows that 'what is right for you may not be right for me.' According to Gene Veith, in his book on postmodernism, 'The best example of an existential ethic can be found in some of those who advocate abortion but call themselves "pro choice". To them, it makes no difference what the woman decides, only that she makes an authen-tic choice whether or not to have the baby. Whatever she chooses is right – for her.'[55] Pro-choice advocates are not interested in any objec-tive moral standard; a woman must decide for herself whether, at that particular time and in those particular circumstances, abortion is the best choice for her.

Techniques of pro-choice counselling

A feature of the pro-choice position is that it does all it can to avoid any discussion of the morality of abortion. The issue is not whether abortion is right or wrong, but about a woman's right to choose. The *Pro-Choice Alliance*, an umbrella group which includes BPAS, Brook,

Marie Stopes International and the Family Planning Association, runs a national campaign entitled *Voice for Choice* which aims to secure for all women in the UK the genuine right to decide for themselves whether or not to continue an unwanted pregnancy. *Education for Choice* is a pro-choice organisation that works to create an environment where young people are equipped to make informed choices about pregnancy and abortion. It promotes the idea that every woman has the right to choose how to deal with an unwanted pregnancy, and that includes a right to choose abortion, which is expressed in the phrase 'pro-choice'. The underlying purpose of pro-choice counselling is to enable a woman to choose abortion free from any moral consideration. In other words, pro-choice counselling seeks to de-moralise abortion in the minds of their clients. The techniques of pro-choice counselling illustrate the subtle way in which abortion is removed from the moral arena.

1. Abortion offered as an option

The major obstacle in the way of the pro-abortion position is a woman's conscience. Most women are instinctively reluctant to have an abortion because they know in their heart of hearts that killing the unborn child in their womb must be wrong. A prime task of pro-choice counselling, therefore, is to conceal the moral objections to abortion. And they do so by referring to abortion as an 'option'. The word option is defined as 'the power or liberty to choose'.[56] For once abortion is turned into an 'option' it is no longer seen as wrongdoing, for there is no question whether an 'option' is right or wrong. So 'options' counselling is not about morality, but about choice. By presenting abortion as an 'option', pro-choice counselling gives a woman the liberty to choose to abort the unborn child. By labelling abortion an 'option' the moral question is pushed out of sight. The issue has been de-moralised, and 'options' counselling makes it appear that the 'option' of abortion and the 'option' of continuing with the pregnancy are moral equivalents. A woman is at liberty to choose either, for 'options' counselling legitimises the choice of abortion.

Yet in the Christian view abortion can never be legitimised because it is against God's law. A Christian cannot present what is wrong in God's eyes as an option, for to do so is encouraging a woman to sin against God. Options counselling is deceptive because it covers over the immorality of abortion. Most women, if warned that abortion is wrong, would not accept it as a legitimate choice. To make it such, is surely to suppress the truth, invent something evil, and to approve of those who ignore God's righteous laws *(Romans 1.18, 32)*. Assessed biblically, options counselling is foolishness, for God cannot be mocked. We reap what we sow.

2. Non-directive advice

According to pro-choice counselling there is no moral distinction between the three options (parenting, adoption, abortion), and therefore a woman must decide for herself which option is right for her and it does not matter which she chooses. Only the woman can decide what is best for her, what is right in her eyes, and nobody must interfere with her decision. It is wrong for anyone to attempt to persuade her against abortion – it is wrong for anyone, and especially a pregnancy counsellor, to try to force their moral beliefs on her. According to pro-choice dogma, to persuade a woman to choose one option above another is 'moralising' – imposing one's own moral views on another person. To tell a woman that abortion is wrong is judgemental. It follows that abortion counselling must be non-directive and non-judgemental so that a woman makes her own decision – one with which she feels able to live. And whatever choice she makes, even if the decision is to abort her unborn child, pro-choice counselling supports her decision.

Non-directive counselling is inconsistent with the Christian faith. The Bible is the most directive book in the world. The whole purpose of Christ's ministry is to direct people to God's Truth. He is so directive that He declares Himself to be the only way to God. He directs us to seek first the kingdom of Heaven; He directs us to enter by the narrow gate that leads to life, and He warns that the broad gate leads to destruction. And the Bible is the most judgemental book in the world. God commands all people everywhere to repent, for He has set a day when He will judge the world *(Acts 17.30-31)*. The Bible declares that all men will stand before the judgement throne of God when His righteous judgement will be revealed. 'To those who are self-seeking and do not obey the truth, but obey unrighteousness – indignation and wrath' *(Romans 2.8)*. And Jesus is judgemental. He says that those who cause others to sin face a judgement worse than a millstone around the neck and being cast into the sea. He condemns those who on the outside appear to be righteous but on the inside are full of hypocrisy.

The Christian who is faithful to God's Word cannot ignore the directive, judgemental message of the Bible. The Christian who is serving Jesus cannot give non-directive, non-judgemental, non-biblical advice regarding abortion. Jesus said: 'For whoever is ashamed of Me and My words, of him the Son of Man will be ashamed when He comes in His own glory . . .' *(Luke 9.26)*. We have a God-given responsibility to warn the individual and society that the Bible teaches that abortion is wrong. God hates hands that shed innocent blood, and Christians have a duty to declare this truth. We cannot give non-directive advice while the innocents are being led to the slaughter. We must warn of the serious consequences of ignoring God's law, and we will be held to account if we fail *(Ezekiel 3.17-18)*. Those Christians who would be faithful to God's Word have a duty to warn against the evil of abortion.

3. Morality based on feelings

Pro-choice counselling believes that a woman's feelings are the best guide to her decision. Because there is no objective moral standard to guide her decision-making, a woman must turn to her subjective, changing emotions. The guiding principle is how she feels about having an abortion. The most important thing is that she feels comfortable with her decision – that she feels able to live with her decision. Whatever she feels is best for her, whatever feels comfortable, and whatever feels convenient at the time, that is what's right for her. In this way a woman is encouraged to believe that her subjective feelings are paramount, and the life of the unborn child is dispensable.

The Christian position is to explain that moral decisions should be based on God's Word. The psalmist declared, 'Through Your precepts I get understanding; therefore I hate every false way. Your word is a lamp to my feet and a light to my path . . . The entirety of Your word is truth, and every one of Your righteous judgments endures forever' *(Psalm 119.104-105, 160)*. Christ said that everyone who hears His words and puts them into practice is like a wise man who builds his house on the rock. When the storms of life come, the house built on the solid rock of God's Word will stand. The foolish man is the one who does not put the words of Jesus into practice. His house is built on the shifting sand of human feelings. When the storms come, as they surely will, the house built on human emotions will fall with a great crash.

4. Informed choice

Pro-choice counselling promotes the idea that the best way for a woman to decide between the options set before her is for her to make an 'informed choice'. As there is no objective moral standard to guide her decision-making, she is invited to make an entirely personal decision on the basis of how she sees things. It is important that she makes her own choice, and is not influenced by judgemental moralising. She is provided with lots of morally neutral information so that she can weigh up the pros and cons of each option. In effect she can calculate a profit and loss account to help her decide which option delivers the greatest net benefits. According to CARE, a woman seriously considering abortion is most helpfully assisted by a quiet caring offer to look at all the facts relating to her decision. 'Facts and effect of termination can be explored sensitively with the counsellee and counsellor looking at the information together.'[57] The more information she has about each option the better chance she has of making a decision she can live with.

She makes a pragmatic 'informed' choice which is the right one for her.

During the last few decades the concept of 'informed choice' has become an integral part of virtually all family planning, abortion counselling and sex education programmes worldwide. The term 'informed choice' first appeared in family planning literature in the early 1970s.[58] In 1987, the Task Force on Informed Choice, which included the International Planned Parenthood Federation (IPPF), met to develop guidance on how 'informed choice' should be used in family planning programmes.[59] In 1994, the International Conference on Population and Development (Cairo) agreed that informed choice in family planning is based on human rights.

The IPPF has a deep commitment to the concept of 'informed choice'. According to an annual programme review: 'The commitment of the IPPF towards empowering young people to make informed decisions and choices regarding their sexual and reproductive health has been solid and unwavering since the early 1990s.'[60] In 2002 the IPPF called on the United Nations Special Session for Children to stand by its previous commitments to young people's sexual rights. Dr Pramilla Senanyake of the IPPF said: 'We believe that with the tools to make "informed choices", young men and women can not only protect themselves from the risks of HIV, unwanted pregnancy and unsafe abortion, they can also enjoy a better life with the freedom to achieve their aspirations.'[61]

The Christian position is that man's life should be directed by God's Word. The Bible warns of the folly of thinking that we can go our own way. The prophet Jeremiah declared: 'O Lord, I know the way of man is not in himself; it is not in man who walks to direct his own steps' *(Jeremiah 10.23)*. We have already seen that moral decisions are to be made on the basis of God's law as contained in His Word, not on the basis of spurious facts, unstable emotions and changing circumstances. The problem with the 'informed' choice is that it is an amoral choice – that is, a choice that flies in the face of God's moral law. It promotes the idea that we can direct our own steps, make our own choices without reference to God's Word. It misleads a vulnerable woman into believing that she is free to choose to abort her unborn child without facing the inevitable consequences of breaking God's moral law.

Endnotes

1 British Pregnancy Advisory Service (BPAS) leaflet, *Unplanned pregnancy: your choices.*

2 Planned Parenthood Federation of America website, health information/ pregnancy/what if I'm pregnant?

3 Pro-choice Connection website, Identifying your feelings.

4 National Abortion Federation leaflet, *Unsure about your pregnancy? A guide to making the right decision for you*, written by Terry Beresford.

5 CARE Centres Network website, It's positive – what are my options?

6 Ibid. BPAS leaflet

7 Ibid. BPAS leaflet.

8 Ibid. Planned Parenthood Federation of America website.

9 Planned Parenthood Alberta website, Be Aware of Anti-choice, Questions to ask to ensure you are talking to a pro-choice organisation.

10 Irish Family Planning Association website, Pregnancy Counselling, Un-planned pregnancy, how we can help you.

11 Ibid. National Abortion Federation leaflet.

12 Ibid. Pro-choice Connection website, Reviewing the Options.

13 CARE, *Making a Decision* leaflet, It's a positive pregnancy test result, p 2.

14 Ibid. Losses and gains, p 2.

15 CARE Centres Network website, It's positive – what are my options?

16 CARE*confidential* website, Services we offer.

17 Ibid. BPAS leaflet.

18 FPA website, FPA policy statement on abortion.

19 Irish Family Planning Association website, How can you be sure you are pregnant?

20 Ibid. Planned Parenthood Alberta website, Questions to ask to ensure you are talking to a pro-choice organisation.

21 Brook website, press release, 20 April 2004, Brook supports access to the facts of abortion.

22 Marie Stopes International, UK press release, 21 February 2002.

23 Ibid. *Unsure about your pregnancy?* Do you need more information?

24 CARE Centres Network website, Making a decision.

25 CARE*confidential* website, leaflet, More about CARE*confidential.*

26 Hull Crisis Pregnancy Centre website.

27 Ibid. BPAS leaflet.

28 Ibid. Irish Family Planning Association website.

29 Ibid. Pro-choice Connection website, Talking the issue over.

30 Ibid. National Abortion Federation leaflet, *Unsure about your pregnancy?*

31 CARE Centres Network website, Abortion.

32 Ibid. BPAS leaflet.

33 Ibid. Irish Family Planning Association website.

34 Ibid. *Making a Decision*, p 3.

35 Prochoiceforum website, Practice issues, Abortion counselling: issues and approaches by Gill Holden, Deborah Russell and Catherine Paterson.

36 Ibid. Planned Parenthood Alberta website, The Option of Abortion.

37 Brook website, news 20 April 2002.

38 Marie Stopes booklet, Abortion, your questions answered.

39 BBC World Service website, Global News and Comment, Sexwise, project overview.

40 CARE, *Called to Care*, Pregnancy counselling, p 77.

41 CARE Centres Network website, Making a decision.

42 CARE Centres Network website, Men and Crisis Pregnancy.

43 CARE*confidential* website, leaflet, More About CARE*confidential*.

44 Ibid. BPAS leaflet.

45 Ibid. Planned Parenthood Federation of America, website, How can I be sure I'm pregnant?

46 Ibid. Planned Parenthood Federation of America, website, How can I decide which choice is best for me?

47 Ibid. Pro-choice Connection website, Making a Decision and committing to it.

48 Ibid. *Making a Decision*, p 4.

49 CARE Centres Network website, Abortion.

50 CARE Centres Network website, Making a decision.

51 Ibid. *Called to Care*, Pregnancy counselling, p 92.

52 The Living Church, 18 July, 1965, cited from *Whatever happened to sex*, Mary Whitehouse, Hodder and Stoughton, London, p 10-11.

53 Joseph Fletcher, *Situation Ethics*, 1966, p 139.

54 Joseph Fletcher, *The Ethics of Genetic Control*, Anchor Press, New York, 1974, pp 119, 121.

55 Gene Edward Veith, *Guide to Contemporary Culture*, Crossway Books, reprinted 1996, p 38.

56 Collins English Dictionary, Millennium Edition, HarperCollins Publishers, 1999.

57 Ibid. *Called to Care*, Pregnancy counselling, p 88.

58 Family Planning Programs, Population Reports, Series J, Number 50, volume XXIX, Number 1, Spring 2001, Population Information Program, The Johns Hopkins University Bloomberg School of Public Health, Informed

Choice, Evolution of Informed Choice.

59 Ibid. Population Reports, Series J, Number 50, Evolution of Informed Choice.

60 IPPF, Annual Programme Review 2002-2003, Young people, p 61.

61 IPPF website, Stand by your commitment to adolescents, IPPF urges, 1 May 2002.

3
CARE's Counselling on the Ground

WHILE A KEY ASPECT of pro-choice dogma is to present abortion as an option, the duty of the church as 'the pillar and ground of the truth' is to teach and proclaim that abortion is against God's moral law. Disciples of Christ are the salt of the earth and the light of the world. A light is put on a lampstand so that it gives light to everybody in the house. 'Let your light so shine before men, that they may see your good works and glorify your Father in heaven' *(Matthew 5.13-16).*

The apostle Paul developed this theme when he referred to Christians as children of the light who should have nothing to do with the unfruitful deeds of darkness but rather expose them. He further commanded believers to put on the full armour of God in order to stand against the devil's schemes, which include the subtle deception of pro-choice counselling. Because we are involved in a spiritual battle, we should use the Word of God as our weapon against the spiritual forces of darkness *(Ephesians 5.8; 6.11-12, 17).*

God's perfect moral law

It is only when we understand God's moral law, as contained in God's Word, that we understand the true nature of abortion. Only God's Word can explain why abortion is a moral issue of such importance. It is because human beings are created in the image of God that human life, including the life of the unborn child, is of overwhelming value in God's eyes. The sanctity of human life and the protection of the innocent, two pillars of Western civilisation, are essential principles that flow from God's moral law. Because human beings are created in the image of God, all men and women are moral beings with a sense of moral obligation. God's laws are righteous and for all people, for all time – they are the laws by which all people ought to live. The Ten Commandments, which express God's holy character, are the summary of the eternal, objective standard of righteous conduct. According to the psalmist 'The law of the Lord is perfect, converting the soul; the testimony of the Lord is sure, making wise the simple; the statutes of the Lord are right, rejoicing the heart; the commandment of the Lord is pure, enlightening the eyes; the fear of the Lord is clean, enduring forever; the judgments of the Lord are true and righteous altogether' *(Psalm 19.7-9)*.

God's law reveals the justice, truth, compassion, faithfulness, and purity that are essential attributes of His character. Every person has a duty to God to obey His law, and God has set a time when all mankind will be judged by His law. Our Lord explained that the commandments of God pertain to our attitudes and desires, as well as our actions. The sixth commandment forbids not only murder but also an attitude of hatred towards others. Because of our moral nature, as created in the image of God, we have a sense of right and wrong, for God has written His law into the heart of man, and no one is free from the inner sense of right and wrong. The apostle Paul makes it clear that even those who do not have the law show that its requirements, which bear witness to this inner sense of right and wrong, are written on their hearts and their consciences *(Romans 2.15)*. In his book *Conscience*, Professor Ole Hallesby writes: 'We can, therefore, define conscience as that knowledge or consciousness by which man knows that he is conforming to moral law or the will of God . . . it is an awareness of a holy, superhuman law which addresses itself to man's conscious will, not in order to enforce its requirements, but that man might follow it freely without compulsion. In fact, it is through conscience that man acquires consciousness of his humanity and is thus distinguished from the brute.'[1]

The issue of abortion is one of the great moral questions of our time. While the Abortion Act of 1967 legalised abortion on certain grounds, most people know in their conscience that abortion is wrong. A woman with an unplanned pregnancy therefore faces a moral dilemma, for while abortion may have been legalised by the British Government, God's Word and her conscience warn her that abortion is wrong. And because she is created in the image of God, and has God's law written on her heart, she knows that she is responsible for her actions. She also has a maternal instinct that makes it natural to love the child in her womb. She knows that the new life in her womb is an act of procreation. It is God's will that a mother should protect and nurture her child. Most women recognise that children are a gift from God *(Psalm 127.3)*.

So a woman with an unplanned pregnancy must make a moral decision whether she follows her conscience and keeps the baby or whether she ignores her conscience and aborts the baby. A great number of women with unplanned pregnancies are being encouraged by non-judgemental options counselling to deaden their consciences and follow the whims and notions of their own wishes, putting their own feelings before what is right. These women need help and guidance from God's Word to awaken their consciences. They need to understand why abortion, the shedding of innocent blood, is such a grave sin, and why the life of the unborn child should be protected. The techniques of pro-choice counselling are designed to persuade a woman to ignore the moral dimension and thereby silence her conscience.

CARE's guidance for pregnant women

We now turn to CARE's approach to pregnancy counselling. What does this mean on the ground? What advice do Christian counsellors give to those women who seek their help? Four examples of the advice provided by CARE's network of counselling centres are presented below:

1. The Hull Crisis Pregnancy Counselling Centre

The Hull Centre, with the slogan 'offering care, compassion and practical support' is a fairly typical example of a crisis pregnancy centre that is part of CARE's network. It has a particularly informative website that explains its services as follows: 'We are a Christian organisation working in the sensitive area of unplanned pregnancy/abortion, and some clients may have concerns as to the nature of our information. Our aim is to enable a client to make an "informed choice" regarding the pregnancy, having reviewed all the options, that it parenting, abortion, adoption, with full information given. Some client feedback from users of the Centre includes: "Thanks for providing such an important service and for not pressurising anyone into any one option." And, "The three options were explained very clearly and 'unbiasedly', which was extremely nice and helpful, with no bias toward any option."'[2]

A woman who enters the website will find the following advice: 'Sometimes, finding you are unexpectedly pregnant can be a difficult and confusing experience. Maybe you are faced with choices that have no easy answers. At the centre you can talk to a trained counsellor who will listen, offer you space to think and help you consider the possible options: parenting, abortion, adoption. Continuing with an unplanned pregnancy may have financial, relationship, housing or career implications. We will help you find the answers you need in order for you to make an informed decision about the future of your pregnancy.'[3]

With regard to abortion the website has this advice: 'Termination of pregnancy can be a difficult decision for some people and we aim to support individuals/couples and provide information that will help them to make an informed choice. If requested, information can be provided concerning the abortion procedures involved but this is handled sensitively and with compassion . . . A woman may feel surrounded by people all telling her what she should or should not do but we aim to encourage her to search and discover what it is she really wants to do so that her decision is one that is right for her.'[4]

Hull Crisis Pregnancy Centre stresses: 'We are here to help people work through pregnancy related issues in a non-judgemental way. As a Christian faith based organisation we always offer help and ongoing support whatever the decision the client makes regarding an unplanned pregnancy.' Moreover, 'here at the Centre we appreciate that none of the options are easy ones to choose – each has its own pros and cons. However, we do believe that if a client makes a well thought through informed decision about the future of the pregnancy, rather than a rushed panic decision, then they are more likely to make the choice that is right for them.'[5]

The Centre also provides advice on emergency contraception. 'If you've had unprotected sex, or a contraceptive device has failed and you do not want to become pregnant – what next, what do you do? Time is crucial, it depends on when the unprotected sex took place as to the choices available.' Choice A is the morning-after pill: 'This must be taken as soon as possible after unprotected sex, but no later than 72 hours.' Choice B is the copper coil: 'This must be fitted within 5 days of unprotected sex.' Finally, 'remember the sooner you obtain emergency contraception, the more effective it will be. Always discuss the best option for you with your GP or other health professional.' While the Centre does not itself provide contraception it does advise its clients of the opening times of Family Planning Clinics where contraceptive advice and supplies can be obtained. With regard to sexually transmitted diseases clients are told that 'the only way to enjoy entirely safe sex is to only have one sexual partner who has not had a previous sexual relationship.'[6]

The Hull Centre not only provides pro-choice pregnancy counselling, it also provides advice on emergency contraception. Note how the non-judgemental, options counselling strives to help a woman make an informed choice that is right for her. Note also the entire absence of any moral guidance. In what way does this guidance differ from that provided by the pro-choice organisations?

2. Northern Ireland Crisis Pregnancy Counselling Centre

The Northern Ireland Crisis Pregnancy Counselling website encourages a woman with an unplanned pregnancy to 'think about your feelings and values before coming to a decision'.[7] The website, based on CARE's leaflet *Making a Decision*, advises a woman with a positive pregnancy test that she has three options. 'When you're ready, you and your husband or partner will need to consider the options available: parenting, adoption or abortion. You may already have a clear idea about what is best for you, or you may have conflicting feelings.' Note that the objective is what's best for the woman, not what's right. There is no acknowledgement that abortion is a moral issue. And to make sure that the woman is not influenced by the views of other people the website is careful to emphasise: 'Although the decision ahead of you may be one of the most difficult you'll ever have to make, it must be your decision and no-one else's.'[8] Most pro-choice counselling programmes stress this point because they do not want the woman to be swayed by the 'moralisers' who may try to persuade her to keep the baby.

So how does a woman decide what is best for her? The first thing for her to consider is her circumstances. 'Circumstances can make an unplanned pregnancy hard to face. That's often because we are afraid of losing things that are important to us; not just practical things like time and money, but things like freedom, peace of mind, and relationships. You may be afraid that you won't cope with having a baby, particularly if it means having a larger family to care for. Your partner or husband may feel unsure about the situation too. Perhaps you feel your marriage or relationship wouldn't take the strain of a new baby.

Or you may feel you are too young or have no support. It's also hard not to be concerned about what others would think.' Here the woman is persuaded that she must consider her particular circumstances in order to decide what the best thing is for her. In other words, what is the pragmatic solution in view of her particular situation? This way of thinking is usually referred to as situation ethics.

It's important for a woman to remember that she has the right to choose. 'Sometimes it's hard to make choices. That's because we often gain something but lose something as well. With each of the options open to you, there are gains and losses involved.' So how does she go about calculating her gains and losses? Well, the sensible thing is to make a list. 'Write a list of those things you think you might lose with each of the options. These may include things like money, accommodation, time, freedom, and the baby itself, but also other things like self-worth, peace of mind, and sense of security.' That is, a woman is advised to consider her gains and losses in economic and psychological terms. If she allows the pregnancy to continue she will most probably lose money, because she will be unable to work for a time, and the baby costs money to feed and clothe. The baby will undoubtedly restrict her social life, she might have to give up education and she might even lose her accommodation. So continuing with the pregnancy can be very costly indeed. If she chooses abortion, on the other hand, the only thing she probably stands to lose is the baby.

Now she must write a list of the things she will gain. 'This time, go through the list and think of the things you would gain with each of the options. How important are these gains to you?' She may well be inclined to think that if she continues with the pregnancy the only thing she stands to gain is the baby, which costs money and restricts her freedom. And what does she gain from abortion? Well, she certainly no longer has the baby she may not want, and she also benefits financially. From her carefully constructed balance sheet she is now in a position to make a trade-off between her losses and gains.

It is not difficult to see that what is being promoted is pure situation ethics. We have already seen the father of situation ethics, Joseph Fletcher, describe his approach to ethical decisions: 'Most of us decide for or against things on the principle of proportionate good. We try to figure out the gains and losses that would follow from one course of action or another and then choose the one that is best, the one that offers the most good. This calculation of consequences is often called a trade-off or cost-benefit analysis.'[9] So the guidance offered by the Northern Ireland website is consistent with the teaching of Joseph Fletcher, and has nothing to do with biblical morality. And this is no small matter. What is at stake is the life of the unborn child, and all that CARE has to offer is an appeal to situation ethics.

The website reminds the woman that in a state of panic it is very difficult to know what she should do. This is why she should consult her subjective feelings for guidance. 'Ask yourself what your instinctive feelings are about each option: keeping the baby, placing the baby for adoption, or having an abortion.' Now a woman must decide what she feels about abortion and having a baby. 'If you detect any instinctive feelings, try and think what it is about that option that makes you feel that way.' For example, does she feel that abortion is right or wrong? Or does she feel that the foetus in her womb is just a blob of multiplying cells? Or does she feel that a baby only becomes human after it's born? Or perhaps she feels that as lots of women are having abortions why shouldn't she? And if she feels that way, then abortion seems a rather sensible, pragmatic solution to her problem.

It is important for the woman to be honest about her feelings and personal values. 'We can allow our instinctive feelings and the awareness of personal values to surface or we can suppress them. When we don't acknowledge deeper feelings either consciously or unconsciously, it's called denial . . . you need to be totally honest with yourself, how you feel about keeping the baby, placing the baby for adoption or having an abortion before you make a final decision.'

And now the woman must make a choice. 'You've weighed up what each option means to you in terms of the losses and gains you might experience. You've questioned whether those losses really will happen or not. You've also checked whether any deeper feelings or personal values are not being acknowledged . . . Make sure you have read all the factual information about each option before you make a final decision. Having looked at all the facts and explored thoroughly how you feel about each option, you may be ready to make your decision. It's important that you feel able to live with the decision you have made.' As with pro-choice counselling, she is advised that the crucial thing in her decision is that she is able to live with it. What she wants is paramount, and as long as she feels she can live with abortion then that makes it a sensible choice.

'If you need further help, CARE in Crisis can offer trained counsellors that are available to give you additional information to help you explore your feelings further. We would welcome your husband or partner as well. This is a free and confidential service.' What is so depressing about this advice is that it is devoid of any moral guidance. CARE has effectively de-moralised abortion by offering advice based on the principles of situation ethics. How sad that a woman is advised to construct a gains-and-losses account to help her decide whether her unborn child is worth keeping.

3. Choices Pregnancy Counselling Centre, Ealing

Choices Pregnancy Counselling Centre was opened in 1999 in West Ealing. According to its website 'its team of volunteers are people with Christian beliefs and values who are deeply concerned that women are enabled to make the best choices for themselves based on non-judgemental, balanced information. We are not a medical centre, so we do not provide contraception or abortion services ourselves, but we provide contraception information leaflets and refer people on to family planning clinics and their GP when appropriate.'[10]

The centre also provides advice on emergency contraception. 'If you've had unprotected sex, or a contraceptive device has failed and you do not want to become pregnant, what can you do? Time is crucial. The morning after pill must be taken *as soon as possible* after unprotected sex, but no later than 72 hours. This is 95% effective. It is available from your GP, Family Planning Clinic, most Sexual Health Clinics and some Pharmacists . . . Remember, the sooner you obtain emergency contraception, the more effective it will be. Please note that Choices does not provide any form of contraception, but we would be happy to discuss these options with you.'[11]

For the woman with a positive pregnancy test the centre has this advice: 'You may well be feeling shocked and wishing you could go back to before you were pregnant. However, nothing can change the fact of your pregnancy, you can only move on and make a decision that you will be able to live with . . . You may feel under pressure, or that there is only one choice. This decision could be one of the most important of your life, so give yourself time. If you act against your personal values, you may well experience guilt at a later stage, which can lead to other problems. Think through these questions, not just in terms of money or time, but also about your peace of mind and how your relationships may be affected. Look at the sections below on continuing the Pregnancy, Adoption and Abortion.

- What makes a pregnancy difficult at the moment?
- What will I lose or gain if I have an abortion?
- What will I lose or gain if I keep the baby?
- What will I lose or gain if I have the baby adopted?

These are difficult questions. Choices provides trained counsellors who can help you think about the way ahead.'[12]

The option of continuing with the pregnancy is raised. 'You may already have dismissed this as an option. Under difficult circumstances, many women feel that way. Having a baby can mean a big responsibility. It is hard work. There may be financial difficulties, housing problems. You would need to consider your loss of freedom and issues related to your career, as well as all the challenges of single parenthood. Many feel that they just couldn't cope. Difficult circumstances can feel overwhelming. You may be worried about the reaction of your partner, your family and your friends. Often the views of the people closest to us affect how we feel. It's important that you consider what you feel about having a baby.'[13]

With regard to abortion the website gives this advice: 'When faced with the difficult situation of an unplanned pregnancy, abortion can seem to be the best choice. But many people know very little about it. You need more information to be able to make this very important decision.'

The centre also provides advice on sexually transmitted diseases. 'Choosing to have sex with someone may bring a risk of being infected with a disease which could lead to infertility, chronic ill-health or a life-threatening condition. Sexually Transmitted Infections, known as STIs, are on the increase . . .' Those who want more detailed information on these infections are referred to the website *playingsafely*.[14] This website, strong on the 'safer sex' message, provides this advice: 'Carry condoms with you when you're out having fun at parties, clubs or with a Valentine, because whether you're planning on it or not you could end up having sex.'[15]

Detailed information is provided on a range of contraceptives. Following a brief description of the pill, the mini pill and the intrauterine device among others, the client is referred to the website of the Family Planning Association for more information on contraception.[16]

The centre is so committed to promoting contraception and emergency contraception that it actually provides an internet link to the Family Planning Association. Notice also the link to the *playingsafely* website which treats sex as no more than a game. But why does a Christian organisation see the need to refer people to such a website?

4. The Glastonbury Pregnancy Counselling Centre

The aim at the Pregnancy Crisis Care Centre is 'to provide a caring relationship, within agreed boundaries, that reflects our Christian commitment, values and understanding'.[17] Trained advisors offer: free pregnancy testing, free confidential counselling, post-abortion counselling, practical help and emotional support. In addition, information and leaflets are available on conventional and emergency contraception, abortion, sexual health matters and adoption and fostering.[18]

Comment

What is deeply disturbing is that CARE Centres are giving the same advice as secular family planning clinics, and that they do so in the name of the Christian church. It seems that these Centres are content to act as outposts for the Government's 'safer sex' ideology. Our Lord warned the church in Thyatira. 'These things says the Son of God . . . I have a few things against you, because you allow that woman Jezebel, who calls herself a prophetess, to teach and beguile My servants to commit sexual immorality . . .' (Revelation 2.18, 20).

What is so sad is that desperate women who turn to a Christian organisation in their hour of need are given advice that is based on the spirit of the age. What all these examples have in common is that they are devoid of moral guidance. God's moral law is simply ignored as irrelevant. It is as if the Bible, which contains wisdom from above, does not exist. Rather than explain why abortion is wrong, women are encouraged to make a pragmatic choice based on their feelings. It is a terrible wrong that such advice should be given by secular clinics, but is it not worse for it to be given by church-based centres?

Endnotes

1 Ole Hallesby, Conscience, Inter-Varsity Press, First published in Christian Classics 1995, pp 8-9.
2 Heros website, Hull and East Riding, Crisis pregnancy centre.
3 Hull Crisis Pregnancy Centre website, Pregnancy testing.
4 Ibid.
5 Ibid. Heros website, Crisis pregnancy centre.
6 Ibid. Hull Crisis Pregnancy Centre website, Information on emergency contraception.
7 Care In Crisis website, Northern Ireland.
8 Ibid. Love for life.

9 Joseph Fletcher, *The Ethics of Genetic Control*, Anchor Press, New York, 1974, pp 119, 121.

10 Ealing Choices Pregnancy Counselling Centre website.

11 Ibid.

12 Ibid.

13 Ibid.

14 Ibid.

15 Playingsafely website.

16 Ibid. Ealing Choices website.

17 Glastonbury Pregnancy Counselling Centre website.

18 Ibid.

.

4

'Called to Care'
A Manual for Christian Pregnancy Crisis Counselling

W
E ARE NOW in a position to make an assessment
regarding CARE's pro-life credentials. Is CARE's pregnancy counselling consistent with its Chairman's claim
that one of 'our strongest passions is to defend the dignity and sanctity
of human life itself'? Is CARE being faithful to their 'responsibility as
Christians to be a voice for the voiceless, because they are defenceless,
and because God alone gave them life'?

The above analysis suggests that the advice provided by CARE's
network of pregnancy counselling centres exhibits all the essential
characteristics of pro-choice dogma. Like pro-choice, CARE's counselling promises to help a pregnant woman find out what she wants to do
about her pregnancy. Like pro-choice, CARE's counselling offers a
woman three options, including abortion. Like pro-choice, CARE's
counselling is impartial, non-judgemental and non-directive. Like pro-
choice, CARE's counselling encourages a woman to examine her
feelings. A pregnant woman is advised to 'think about your feelings
and values before coming to a decision'. CARE's leaflet, *Making a*

Decision, uses the words feel or feelings over twenty times. Like pro-choice, CARE's counselling helps a woman clarify her personal values. Like pro-choice counsellors, CARE's counsellors invite a woman to make an 'informed' choice between the options that have been set before her. Like pro-choice counsellors, CARE's counsellors persuade a woman that the most important thing is that she feels able to live with her choice. Is there, in reality, any difference between the non-directive, non-judgemental, options-based counselling of CARE and the pro-choice, non-directive, non-judgemental, options-based counselling of BPAS, Planned Parenthood, Pro-choice Connection, National Abortion Federation and Marie Stopes?

Many supporters of CARE will be dismayed at the thought that it is being bracketed together with pro-choice abortion organisations. There is something profoundly wrong here. Either CARE's position is being misrepresented or it has departed from the faith that was once for all entrusted to the saints, and is promoting, or at least condoning, abortion in the name of the Christian church. This is a serious accusation that demands an answer. To consider the question of whether CARE has departed from the biblical faith, we need to examine the theological justification for its pregnancy counselling. We need to understand the theology that lies behind CARE's ministry of non-judgemental, options counselling.

Called to Care, first produced in 1994 and revised in 2002, attempts to provide the biblical basis for CARE's position on pregnancy counselling. It is a training manual for Christians who wish to become counsellors in CARE's network of counselling centres. It is also intended for teachers, church workers, social workers and others in the caring professions who want to increase their skills in the area of counselling pregnant women.

A secular model of counselling

Called to Care makes it clear that its counselling process is based on the model of psychologist Gerard Egan. 'It is a secular model but gives the interviewing/counselling a structure without violating any biblical principles and leaves plenty of room for the Holy Spirit to work.'[1] At the heart of the counselling process is the idea of empathy which can be basic or advanced. 'Basic empathy is the skill used to communicate to another person that we have understood the way they see the situation and how they feel about it . . . Basic empathy is reflected when the counsellor understands what the counsellee feels and why.'[2] Advanced empathy is defined as 'sharing hunches about clients; to perceive accurately feelings and meanings which are hidden to, or unformulated by the client.'[3] The counsellor helps a woman draw logical conclusions from what she is saying. For example, 'From what you have said, it seems as though you resent remaining with your husband. I know you haven't actually said that, but I wonder if that is how you are feeling?'[4]

The counsellor is reminded that she is there 'to help them make an informed choice'.[5] According to the manual, as humans 'we can repress, suppress or otherwise inhibit feelings'. While acknowledging that its counselling technique is 'borrowed from secular psychology', the manual claims that the principles of empathy, genuineness, unconditional acceptance and humility are based on biblical principles.[6]

A counsellor is advised: ' . . . with the help of the Holy Spirit, when you put intellectual facts together with feelings you will understand what the woman feels and why she feels as she does and you will experience compassion/empathy for her. The Bible does not use the word empathy; instead it uses the word compassion. For example, the response of the father to the prodigal son in *Luke 15.20*: "But while he was still a long way off, his father saw him and was filled with compassion for him; he ran to his son, threw his arms around him and kissed him." Another example is in *Matthew 9.36*: "When he saw the crowds, he had compassion on them, because they were harassed and helpless, like sheep without a shepherd." '[7]

Flaws of secular humanistic psychology

The claim that the principles of secular psychology do not violate biblical principles is not true. Most secular psychology is based on a false view of man and certainly does not recognise the sinfulness of the human heart. The Bible provides a strong warning that we should not place our trust in man-made teachings, that we should not be taken captive through hollow and deceptive philosophy, which depends on human tradition and the basic principles of this world rather than on Christ *(Colossians 2.8)*. Egan's counselling technique is based on feelings and emotions. It is a human philosophy based on the principles of this world. It is the philosophy that underpins CARE's counselling techniques.

In *Psychology as Religion: the Cult of Self-worship,* Professor Paul Vitz demonstrates the anti-Christian position of secular psychology. He argues that 'psychology has become a religion, in particular, a form of secular humanism based on worship of the self'.[8] Psychology now exists as a deeply anti-Christian religion which 'has for years been destroying individuals, families and communities'.[9] He believes that the recent increases in the rate of marital dissolution owe much to the values advanced by self-theory, for 'such notions as duty and sacrifice are rejected by today's popular self-theory counsellors and therapists'.[10] The basic assumption of humanistic selfism is the complete goodness of human nature; its ability to justify self-indulgence has increased its popularity. The selfish position places a large emphasis 'on empathy and identification with others' and this has led to a reaction against reason and objectivity.[11] 'Historically, selfism derives from an explicitly anti-Christian humanism and its hostility to Christianity is a logical expression of its very different assumptions about the nature of the self, of creativity, of the family, of love, and of suffering. In short, humanistic selfism is not a science but a popular secular substitute religion, which has nourished and spread today's widespread cult of self-worship.'[12]

In *Psychology Gone Awry* Mark Cosgrove draws attention to the flaws in humanistic psychology, the brand of psychology that focuses on a person's feelings and needs. As the counsellor focuses on the individual, so the experiences of the individual become 'truth'. Cosgrove explains, 'Since I am the object of study, that which I experience is being defined as truth, says the humanistic psychologist.'[13] As the humanistic psychologist redefines truth there is no longer an objective reality, for 'experiences and feelings are the prime stuff of reality'.[14] Moreover, the emphasis on moral relativism means that no type of behaviour is labelled as good or bad. 'Once these categories are lost, the strivings for changing people's "sin" nature disappears in psychology.'[15] Instead, humanistic psychology encourages counselling techniques that explore and focus on the self. 'There is a great emphasis on strengthening one's self image . . . and on non-directive, empathetic counselling to rid the self of limiting guilt.'[16] In summary then, 'the humanistic psychologist is often more interested in what his client thinks or feels about something than in absolute truth. For example, what one feels is a valid sexual encounter becomes truth for him or her. This, of course, ends any discussion of absolute truth in the counselling office or the classroom.'[17]

The counselling technique employed by CARE is a classic example of humanistic selfism. Everything is directed towards the wants and needs of the woman. The counselling is designed to appeal to her own desires as it draws her away and entices her with the option of abortion *(James 1.14)*. Empathy and feelings are everything, while objective truth found in God's Word has no place. This approach is light years away from the message of the Bible. Jesus taught His disciples to deny themselves, to take up their cross daily and follow Him *(Luke 9.23)*. The way of the cross is the way of self-denial and sacrifice, putting the interests of others above our own. And why do Christians need to come alongside women with the techniques of secular humanistic psychology when they have the Word of God and the wisdom that is from above? *(James 3.17.)*

Flowing from its psychological mindset, CARE equates the compassion of the father for the prodigal son and the compassion of Jesus for the harassed crowd with the empathy generated by secular psychology.

But this is a fallacious comparison. Empathy is a subjective emotion based on understanding a woman's feelings. Compassion is an objective truth based on God's character. God the Father revealed His compassion for mankind by sending His Son to die on the cross of Calvary, not by understanding our feelings. 'God demonstrates His own love toward us, in that while we were still sinners, Christ died for us' *(Romans 5.8)*. The compassion of Jesus was aroused by the spiritual need of the crowd. And He demonstrated His compassion by commanding His disciples to ask the Lord of the harvest to send out workers into the harvest field to preach the Gospel.

The counselling process

The *Called to Care* manual explains the process of crisis pregnancy counselling. A woman is received and welcomed as an important guest. 'The initiator of the appointment is the Holy Spirit, therefore she is His guest.'[18] Having done a pregnancy test the counsellor should pray, asking God for His peace, and be assured that the Holy Spirit will guide the counsellor. With a positive test the counsellor should say to the woman, 'The tests are very accurate but you will need to have your pregnancy confirmed by your GP. What are you feeling about it?'[19] In the event of a positive test and an unhappy mother the counselling process begins.

Stage 1 is to ascertain how the woman 'sees her situation and what she feels about it . . . We want to help her to feel we fully respect her perception of the situation, and understand her distress.'[20] Stage 2 is to explore the various options. 'When you sense that a good relationship has been established, begin to explore the various options . . . Ask the Holy Spirit to pinpoint areas where the woman has special difficulties, or where she is vulnerable. Try to assess what she is feeling about it, in contrast to what others may feel.'[21] And, 'It is very important to discuss thoroughly all the options available to a woman in a crisis pregnancy situation. She is in a position of being able to choose but may not feel that she has any choice . . . Explain how she has the opportunity to explore all the facts relating to each option . . . It is reasonable and sensible to consider all the options before making a final decision. Begin with the option that she seems to prefer. Enable her to imagine each choice as if there was no alternative.'[22]

'A woman seriously considering abortion in response to her test is most helpfully assisted by a quiet caring offer to look at all the facts relating to her decision . . . Facts and effect of termination can be explored sensitively with the counsellee and counsellor looking at the information together.'[23] Considering the spiritual effects of abortion, 'most people will admit some belief in God and have wondered what He would feel about it: this may give an opportunity to speak about God's boundaries. Be sensitive to the Holy Spirit: often He will give you an opportunity to share about God's love and concern for her and her baby.'[24]

The third stage of the counselling process is to help the woman make her decision. 'She has received all the important information necessary and discussed all her options in depth. She understands more clearly the consequences of each option but now has to decide which set of consequences she is going to give priority. She has to make the decision she can live with.'[25] 'If she is determined to pursue an abortion, refer her to her doctor and assure her that help will be available afterwards in the form of counselling if she needs it.'

Comment

The aim of CARE's counselling is to help a woman reach the stage where she can make an informed choice. Notice how CARE suggests that the Holy Spirit of God is involved in the process – it is the Holy Spirit Who initiates the appointment; it is the Holy Spirit Who guides the counsellor in her non-judgemental, empathetic counselling; it is the Holy Spirit Who helps the counsellor to identify areas where the woman is vulnerable. CARE is making a great play on the idea that God the Holy Spirit is involved with the counselling process, helping women choose between the options. But this is a false view of the Holy

Spirit. 'When He [the Holy Spirit] has come, He will convict the world of sin, and of righteousness, and of judgment' *(John 16.8)*. It is unthinkable that God the Holy Spirit, Who convicts the world of guilt in regard to sin, Who hates hands that shed innocent blood, is a participant in a counselling session that offers abortion as an option. It is unthinkable that the Holy Spirit Who convicts the world of judgement is a participant in non-judgemental counselling. It is unthinkable that the Spirit of truth is a party to options counselling based on the techniques of secular psychology. CARE counsellors are deceiving themselves if they believe that the Holy Spirit has any part in their non-directive counselling sessions.

CARE's view of Jesus Christ

The manual explains that to be 'effective in social action the church must firstly recognise problems in morality and unrighteousness that face our nation and then confront them head on without shying away from the difficult ethical issues. This demands a two-fold response. Firstly we must understand how God feels about each of the issues faced, clearly speaking out God's will and tackling the root of the problem. Secondly we need to reach out to those whose lives have been wrecked and destroyed by the area of sin that we want to redress . . . Whilst God abhors unrighteousness and injustice He also longs to reach out to those who are downcast and broken-hearted.'[26] Indeed, God does abhor unrighteousness and injustice. The Scriptures emphasise that God hates the unrighteous hands that shed innocent blood. God showed His righteous anger when the people of Judah built high places 'to burn their sons and their daughters in the fire', something that God did not command and that was so shocking that it did not enter His mind *(Jeremiah 7.30-31)*. The heart of God reaches out to women and girls, often broken-hearted themselves, who become pregnant, but not in such a way as to compromise His hatred of abortion. And God also reaches out to the downcast, broken-hearted, innocent unborn child facing the threat of abortion.

Called to CARE describes a few examples in the Gospels where we see Jesus in the company of sinners. For example, Jesus dined with tax collectors, and a woman caught in adultery was brought before Him. 'Jesus did not condone the sin but neither did He condemn the sinner . . . There are many other examples in the Gospels where we see Jesus in the company of the worst sinners. Whilst He never condoned any of their actions, His heart was always to reach out towards them in compassion and mercy, never judging them for their sins but always seeking to bring them to a restored life before God . . . There is not one of us who can point an accusing finger at anyone, however grievous their sin may be. Jesus Himself is our example in that He never judged anyone but was always merciful towards them. In *John 3.17* we see that God sent His Son into the world not to judge the world but that through Him the world might be saved. If we are to be like Him it is not our place to bring judgement to the world but rather to reach out to those in need so that they are able to receive God's love. This is the vision of the pregnancy counselling centres affiliated to the CCN.'[27]

Comment

CARE has described the picture of a non-judgemental Jesus. The heart of Jesus 'was always to reach out *[to sinners]* in compassion and mercy, never judging them for their sins but always seeking to bring them to a restored life before God'. According to CARE, 'He never judged anyone but was always merciful towards them.' The implication of CARE's non-judgemental view of Jesus, seen in the context of abortion counselling, is that He will not judge or condemn those women who choose to abort their unborn children.

Most Christians know that this is a false view of Jesus Christ, for the Bible teaches that God the Father has given all judgement to the Son; Jesus has been given 'authority to execute judgment' *(John 5.22, 27)*. The apostles were commanded to testify that Jesus is 'ordained by God to be Judge of the living and the dead' *(Act 10.42)*. Jesus said: 'I say to you that for every idle word men may speak, they will give account of it in the day of judgement. For by your words you will be justified, and by your words you will be condemned' *(Matthew 12.36, 37)*. Jesus said that it would be more bearable on the day of judgment for the land of Sodom and Gomorrah than for those who refused His word *(Matthew 10.15)*. Jesus gives the strongest warning that those who cause others (including vulnerable young women) to sin face a worse judgement than a millstone hung around their neck and being cast into the sea.

CARE's view of God

According to the manual, 'God wants to use each one of us to bring His love to those who do not know Him . . . God's love is compassionate, non-judgemental and does not condemn. This should be reflected in our attitude, no matter how unrighteous the situation described appears to be.'[28]

Comment

Consistent with its mistaken teaching on Jesus, CARE describes the god behind its abortion counselling as compassionate and non-judgemental, a god that does not condemn. In the context of abortion counselling, the inference is that CARE's god supports non-judgemental counselling that offers abortion as an option. And those who make an informed choice to have an abortion need have no fear that they face condemnation because CARE's 'compassionate' god does not condemn. Most Bible-believing Christians will recognise this as an heretical view of God, for the God of the Bible is the Judge of all the earth *(Genesis 18.25)*, Who will judge the world in righteousness and the people with His truth *(Psalm 96.13)*. In God's moral universe all people are accountable for their actions and God has declared a day of judgement when all people will appear before His great throne.

It's important to understand that CARE's justification for its non-judgemental options counselling is built on its non-judgemental view of God. What CARE has done is to subtly replace the true God of the Bible with their false god who winks at abortion, who overlooks evil, and casually offers three options to women with unwanted pregnancies. CARE has constructed a false god who is comfortable with a psychological view of abortion counselling. CARE's false view allows them to embrace pro-choice counselling while still wearing Christian clothes and still reciting Christian prayers. Their false god, who never judges anybody and most certainly not women who make an informed choice to have an abortion, cares nothing for the unborn, always reaching out in mercy towards those who abort unborn children. Their false god offers comfort to hands that shed innocent blood.

To present a non-judgemental view of God to a woman contemplating abortion encourages her to believe that God does not really care if she chooses abortion. The effect of non-judgemental counselling is to create the impression in the mind of a woman that her act of abortion will not be judged. But this is appalling advice, for God hates the action which is contemplated. In this country most women still know that abortion is wrong, and the Bible provides the strongest possible warning for those who deliberately reject God's law. 'For if we sin willfully after we have received the knowledge of the truth, there no longer remains a sacrifice for sins, but a certain fearful expectation of judgment . . . For we know Him who said, Vengeance is Mine, I will repay, says the Lord. And again, The Lord will judge His people. It is a fearful thing to fall into the hands of the living God' (Hebrews 10.26, 27, 30-31). There is wonderful mercy, through Christ, but this must not be offered in order to encourage the breaking of God's law, and this brings us to our next section.

Compassion and boundaries

CARE's attempt to justify its non-judgemental approach is discussed in a section entitled *Compassion and God's boundaries*. Counsellors are taught that the concept of 'compassion and boundaries' is an important foundation for the counselling process. 'Essentially this means knowing what limits (boundaries) God has given us, and then understanding how to help those in crisis compassionately, but without compromising the truth.'[29] Moreover, 'the boundaries in God's Word (rules, principles, commandments, etc) are universal; they apply to everyone, whether or not they believe in God. They are also for our good: even secular society retains some of them otherwise anarchy would result.'[30] *Called to Care* explains that 'the Bible provides us with the boundaries and limits we need. Two particular passages are at the heart of the Ten Commandments in the Old Testament *(Ex 20)* and the Sermon on the Mount in the New Testament *(Matt 5-7)*. Because we are dealing with actual and potential cases of abortion, we need to resolve for ourselves whether it is the taking of an innocent life. Don't take someone else's word for it – make sure it is your own decision.'[31] The point is made that 'although guilt and shame result from overstepping God's boundaries, His grace and power to forgive mean that there is always a way to forgiveness and salvation, even for those who have gone far beyond God's boundaries.'[32] Three scenarios are discussed – compassion without God's boundaries; God's boundaries without compassion; and CARE's preferred option, compassion and God's boundaries.

1. Compassion without God's boundaries

Pregnancy counsellors are told that 'compassion should be at the heart of our counselling just as it was at the heart of Christ's ministry . . . Exercising compassion without respect for God's boundaries changes our goal. We are no longer motivated to do the right thing in God's eyes, but simply to do what seems best for the person being counselled. Our emotions can motivate us to relieve pain rather than seek a solution within God's boundaries. Many pro-abortion and "pro-choice" individuals are motivated by genuine compassion but have disregarded God's absolute values, thus ending up with the wrong solution.'[33]

A false view of compassion

In CARE's eyes the pro-abortionists, who seek to help a woman to abort her unwanted pregnancy, are motivated by genuine compassion.

CARE asks us to believe that it is the pro-choice pregnancy counsellors, using the techniques of secular psychology, who show a woman 'genuine compassion'. Moreover, we have seen that the heart of Jesus is 'always to reach out towards them *[sinners]* in compassion and mercy, never judging them for their sins but always seeking to bring them to a restored life before God'. So in the context of abortion, the heart of Jesus is 'always to reach out toward them *[women who abort their unborn children]* in compassion and mercy, never judging them for their sins . . .' The inference is that God's law can be broken with impunity because Jesus will always reach out in compassion and mercy, never judging those who wilfully commit abortion. This teaching gives a woman a cast iron guarantee that CARE's feeble Jesus will always forgive her if she decides to abort her pregnancy. What is so shocking is that it actually encourages a woman to commit abortion who would be otherwise reluctant to do so. The reality is that CARE's 'compassion' is a licence to commit evil.

God's compassion is totally different from the 'genuine compassion' of the pro-abortionists. The Scriptures teach that God's compassion is especially directed towards the weak, the poor, the fatherless and the broken-hearted. In the situation where a mother is considering aborting her unborn child, God's compassion is directed towards the defenceless, innocent child. As far as the mother is concerned, the compassion of God points her to the narrow way that leads to life, and warns her that the broad way of abortion leads to destruction. For the mother the compassionate thing is to protect her unborn child. For the pregnancy counsellor, true compassion is to explain that God's law forbids abortion.

The Bible teaches that 'whom the Lord loves He corrects' *(Proverbs 3.12)*. And God disciplines us for our own good. God disciplines a mother for her own good, and for the good of her unborn child, and while no discipline seems pleasant at the time, but painful, in the long run it produces a harvest of righteousness and peace *(Hebrews 12.10,11)*. A Christian counsellor will explain that genuine compassion is found in the Lord of Heaven and earth, the Lord Who loves the innocent unborn, and, in order to protect the life of the unborn, has declared abortion wrong. 'The Lord is merciful and gracious, slow to anger, and abounding in mercy ... As a father pities his children, so the Lord pities those who fear Him' *(Psalm 103.8, 13)*. Notice that in God's eyes, it is accepted as natural for a parent to have compassion on their children. Indeed, God illustrates His compassion for His people by the compassion that parents have for their children. It is therefore unthinkable, in God's mind, that a parent would choose to destroy her child. Those who shed innocent blood in defiance of God's law, or encourage others to shed innocent blood, face the wrath of God, for God hates abortion.

2. God's boundaries without compassion

Called to Care warns that there are some people who are concerned about God's boundaries but who do not have compassion. 'A preoccupation with God's boundaries, not balanced by compassion, results in the sort of approach for which Jesus criticised the experts in Old Testament law, saying: "you load people down with burdens they can hardly carry, and you yourselves will not lift one finger to help them." We are not to use a woman's pain to fight a cause, point the finger or judge, however right we may feel it may be. We are there to serve each woman and we can do so confidently because God has given us something to offer.'[34] Note that CARE is there to serve the woman, not the unborn child. And what is it that CARE has to offer each woman it serves? Three options that include killing the unborn! The manual actually contains an illustration to show that those who are preoccupied with God's law not only have no compassion, but are also judgemental and self-righteous.

A false view of God's law

There is an underlying conflict between CARE's non-judgemental theology and the moral law of God. CARE's non-judgemental approach allows a woman to choose between options (keeping the pregnancy and aborting the pregnancy) without making it absolutely clear that abortion is wrong, for non-judgemental counselling, by definition, does not judge or condemn any action or deed, and certainly does not condemn abortion. God's moral law, on the other hand, judges the thoughts, words and actions of men and women and condemns wrongdoing, sin, lawlessness and hands that shed innocent blood. So in God's eyes, abortion is not an option but rebellion against His law.

CARE portrays those who seek to teach God's moral law (pejoratively referred to as being preoccupied with God's boundaries) as being judgemental. They are accused of being like Pharisees who load people down with burdens without lifting a finger to help. And, in the context of abortion, what is the burden that is being created by those who have 'a preoccupation' for the law? Is it not to show from the Scriptures that God hates abortion? And to do so, in CARE's view, shows a lack of compassion for the woman who is considering an abortion. But to vilify those who teach that abortion is wrong as being like the Pharisees is a misrepresentation of the Scriptures. Jesus attacked the Pharisees, not because they were teaching the law of God, but because they were hypocrites, obsessed with the ritual of their traditions and not obeying the spirit of God's law. Jesus called them hypocrites who honoured God with their lips, but whose hearts were far from God. 'For laying aside the commandment of God, you hold the tradition of men . . . All too well you reject the commandment of God, that you may keep your tradition' *(Mark 7.8-9)*. According to Jesus, it is those who set aside the commands of God who are in error, not those who teach God's commandments.

In the Sermon on the Mount, Jesus makes it clear that He did not come to abolish the law or the prophets but to fulfil them. 'For assuredly, I say to you, till heaven and earth pass away, one jot or one tittle will by no means pass from the law till all is fulfilled. Whoever therefore breaks one of the least of these commandments, and teaches men so, shall be called least in the kingdom of heaven; but whoever does and teaches them, he shall be called great in the kingdom of heaven' *(Matthew 5.18-19)*. Here Jesus is emphasising in the strongest possible way that the law of God, when correctly understood, is the God-given standard for human conduct. He is also saying that those who teach the commandments of God will be called great in the kingdom of Heaven. Those who relax the commandments of God will be the least in God's kingdom. One can but wonder what Jesus would say about those who set themselves up as pregnancy counsellors in His name, but are reluctant to teach that killing the unborn is wrong.

3. Compassion and God's boundaries

The approach adopted by *Called to Care* is 'compassion and God's boundaries'. 'This approach should be our goal; it is the way that Jesus worked, loving the individual without ever compromising His Father's word and law. Our aim is to come alongside women and to help them find a way through their crisis, learning to take responsibility for their own lives. God's way is always best. At times it takes faith to believe this, but we can be sure that there is a way through, a way of hope for every woman we meet. (Even if someone oversteps God's boundaries we still extend compassion, but without encouraging them to overstep the boundaries – no matter how painful the situation.)'[35]

God's law and God's compassion

CARE's preferred approach shows a fundamental lack of understanding of the relationship between compassion and God's law. There is a suggestion that those who have compassion for the pregnant mother might be tempted to compromise God's law. But why this potential conflict between compassion and God's law? Because in CARE's eyes, compassion is helping a woman to do as she wants with her pregnancy. As we have seen above, it is the pro-abortionists who are motivated by genuine compassion, while those who teach God's law are portrayed as judgemental. A moral law that condemns the shedding of innocent blood creates a burden for women which 'they can hardly carry'. So CARE's counsellors try to compensate for the compassion that they feel is missing from God's harsh law by developing empathy with their clients. The fallacy of this approach is that it does not recognise the goodness and compassion inherent in God's law.

In a critique of situation ethics, Dave Miller makes the point that 'the Bible simply does not place law and love in contradistinction to each other. In fact, according to the Bible, one cannot love either God or fellow man without law. The only way for an individual to know how to love is to go to the Bible and discern there the specifics of a loving behaviour.' When Paul declared that love is the fulfilling of the law *(Romans 13.10)*, he did not mean that it is possible to love one's neighbour while dispensing with the law, as proposed by the proponents of situation ethics. 'Rather, he meant that when you conduct yourself in a genuinely loving manner, you are automatically acting in harmony with the law (that is, you are not killing, stealing, coveting, bearing false witness, and so on). God, in His laws, defined and pinpointed how to love. To treat any of God's laws as optional, flexible, or occasional is to undermine the very foundations of love.'[36]

The error of CARE's position is that it does not accept that to help a woman see that abortion is wrong, warning her of the serious spiritual and moral dangers, is an act of genuine compassion. Moreover, CARE's belief that God's 'grace and power to forgive mean that there is always a way to forgiveness and salvation, even for those who have gone far beyond God's boundaries' provides a convenient solution to the problem of unwanted pregnancy – a woman can have an abortion, if she really wants one, for there is always a way to forgiveness. Genuine compassion is explaining the three options and informing a woman that if she chooses abortion God is always willing to forgive. And the woman is further reassured that Jesus Himself never judges but is always merciful.[37] So it really does not matter whether she has the abortion or not, because God will forgive her if she does. Based on this false view of God, the 'compassionate' counsellor can offer the woman both an abortion and 'forgiveness' at the same time. CARE's non-judgemental god is ready and willing to forgive every woman who has an abortion, even those who deliberately and knowingly reject God's law. But this is not the way of the God of the Bible, but the way of those who say 'Shall we continue in sin that grace may abound?' *(Romans 6.1.)*

There is, of course, forgiveness for those who truly repent of abortion, acknowledging their sin and wrongdoing before God, for the blood of Jesus cleanses from all sin. And it is often those who know this forgiveness who take the strongest stand against abortion for they have a deep understanding of why abortion is so wrong.

The fact that CARE believes that God's law needs to be modified by the empathetic approach of its counsellors shows that it does not understand that God's moral law, which is based in righteousness and goodness, exercises a powerful appeal to the hearts of men and women. And in our postmodern society there is a growing hunger for truth, for many people know in their conscience that the Bible provides the standard by which they ought to live. Most women with an unplanned pregnancy know in their conscience that abortion is wrong. To have God's Word explained as it relates to the sanctity of human life can be both a great encouragement and also a severe warning. This is true compassion for both the woman with an unplanned pregnancy and also for her unborn child. It is the duty of God's people to give a clear moral lead and to pronounce unequivocally, with all the authority of God's Word, that abortion is wrong.

The Bible teaches that all morality is grounded in the holy character of the God Who made the world and everything in it; all moral distinctions flow from God's moral law. The Bible makes it plain that God's law is for all people, and especially for the irreligious and the unbeliever. The unbelieving world needs to hear the moral law of God just as much as the Christian world does. God's moral law is especially relevant for the woman contemplating abortion. 'Knowing this: that the law is not made for a righteous person, but for the lawless and insubordinate . . . for the unholy and profane, for murderers of fathers and murderers of mothers *[or unborn children]*, for manslayers, for fornicators, for sodomites, for kidnappers, for liars, for perjurers ...' *(1 Timothy 1.9, 10).*

God's moral law serves the purpose of restraining evil and promoting righteousness. The purpose of the sixth commandment is to protect innocent life – it outlaws abortion, acting as a restraint on the shedding of innocent blood. The law also brings people under conviction of wrongdoing and sin, pointing them to their need of salvation through faith. And for believers it is a rule of life, reminding us of how we ought to live.[38]

Endnotes

1 CARE, *Called to Care*, A manual for Christian pregnancy crisis counselling, revised 2002, Section Two, Principles of counselling, p 32.

2 Ibid. p 36.

3 Ibid. p 38.

4 Ibid. p 38.

5 Ibid. p 32.

6 Ibid. p 23.

7 Ibid. p 23.

8 Paul Vitz, *Psychology as Religion: the Cult of Self-worship*, William B. Eerdmans Publishing Co. 1977, p 9.

9 Ibid. p 10.

10 Ibid. pp 35-36.

11 Ibid. p 116.

12 Ibid. p 105.

13 Mark P Cosgrove, *Psychology Gone Awry*, Inter-Varsity Press, revised edition 1982, p 67.

14 Ibid. p 67.

15 Ibid. p 119.

16 Ibid. p 71.

17 Ibid. p 82.

18 Ibid. *Called to CARE*, Section Three, Pregnancy counselling, p 77.

19 Ibid. p 77.

20 Ibid. p 79.

21 Ibid. p 79.

22 Ibid. p 80.

23 Ibid. p 88.

24 Ibid. p 89.

25 Ibid. p 92.

26 Ibid. Section One, Introduction, p 9.

27 Ibid. pp 9-10.

28 Ibid. *Called to Care*, Section One, Introduction, p 10.

29 Ibid. Section Two, Principles of counselling, p 21.

30 Ibid. p 21.

31 Ibid. p 21.

32 Ibid. p 21.

33 Ibid. p 22.

34 Ibid. p 22.

35 Ibid. p 22.

36 Dave Miller, *Situation Ethics*, Apologetics Press, Reason & Revelation, November 2004 - 24[11]:97-103.

37 Ibid. *Called to Care*, Section One, p 9.

38 Louis Berkhof, *Systematic Theology*, The Banner of Truth Trust, 1979, pp 614-15.

5

CARE's Relative Morality
Making the Decision that is Right for Her

IN THE CLOSING chapters of the *Book of Judges*, a period is recorded when Israel departed from God's law and fell into apostasy. We read: 'In those days there was no king in Israel; *everyone did what was right in his own eyes' (Judges 21.25)*. This period was marked by rebellion against God's Word and moral degeneracy as each person decided for himself what was right and wrong. Here in the Old Testament we see an example of what has come to be called post-modernism, when God's law is set aside and each person does what they believe is right in their own eyes. But this is a dangerous philosophy which leads to moral anarchy. According to *Proverbs*: 'There is a way that seems right to a man, but its end is the way of death' *(Proverbs 14.12)*. And Jesus taught that the broad way based on the wisdom of the age leads to destruction. It is the narrow way, based on God's Word, that leads to life.

In the first chapter we saw CARE's Chairman express his concern about abortion. 'We have a responsibility as Christians to be a voice for the voiceless, because they are defenceless.' So how does CARE exercise this responsibility to the voiceless unborn child? What moral guidance does CARE give to a woman considering abortion?

CARE's moral guidance

CARE's website provides the answer:

'An unplanned pregnancy can make us panic. We want to be in charge of our lives again – this can make us rush into decisions without thinking about our deeper feelings. For example, ask yourself what your instinctive feelings about caring for a child, abortion and adoption are. It might be helpful for you to think about how you felt about having a baby, or an abortion or placing a baby for adoption before you found yourself pregnant. What makes you feel that way? What's important to you? What do you believe is right or wrong? You might believe that stealing is wrong, but recycling paper is a good thing. Think about the three options. *Are they right or wrong in your eyes? [My emphasis.]* If we do something that we feel is instinctively wrong for us, we may feel negatively about it later. Do any of the options go against your feelings in this way?'[1]

Here CARE is encouraging a woman to believe that her opinion of right and wrong is important. She is invited to think about the three options and then to decide whether abortion is right or wrong in her eyes. The inference is that if she believes abortion is right it is an acceptable choice. So in CARE's eyes, when it comes to abortion, a woman should be encouraged to do what she feels to be right in her own eyes. Consistent with this ideology, CARE's Hull Network Centre helps a woman 'to search and discover what it is she really wants to do so that her decision is one that is right for her'.[2] What CARE is propagating is a morality that is defined according to one's feelings.

It is not difficult to see that CARE's approach is based in the philosophy of godless, raw postmodernism, in which each woman has her own view of whether abortion is right for her. In this postmodern view people do not acknowledge any moral absolutes. The woman who feels justified in aborting her unborn child is therefore unaware of the immoral nature of her action. The Bible teaches that God's moral law, declared in God's Word, alone decides right and wrong. 'I, the Lord, speak righteousness, I declare things that are right' *(Isaiah 45.19)*. Abortion cannot be presented as an option because it is against God's law. And so we must face up to these questions: Does CARE's careless disregard of biblical truth legitimise the choice of abortion? Is CARE secretly introducing a destructive heresy into the church? Is CARE bringing the way of truth into disrepute? *(2 Peter 2.1-2.)*

CARE and sex education

Although the focus of this book has been pregnancy counselling, it would be a mistake not to draw attention to CARE's sex education programme. We have seen that CARE's teaching on abortion is based in moral relativism. The question is whether this moral relativism translates into its sex education programme. CARE has been involved with sex education since the early 1990s, and in 1994 produced the video *Make Love Last* with the message that it's okay to say 'no' to sex. Moreover we saw in chapter 1 that in an attempt 'to combat the increase in pregnancy testing and abortion referral clinics' many of CARE's centres 'are including preventative work in their support of young people'.[3] CARE appears to be saying that it supports the idea that the way to reduce unwanted teenage pregnancies is to promote contraception among young people.

'Make Love Last'

The video is laced with smutty sexual innuendoes. One character, Randy Factor, asks a group of young people whether they are 'putting it around a bit, you know, dipping your wick'. Randy promotes an exercise programme to make people 'bonking' fit. He uses phrases like, 'You need to get bonking fit'; 'pumping for humping'; 'leg-over time'; 'the more I score the better I score' and 'the sponsored bonk'. In a skit on the TV programme Blind Date, Randy has his game-show called Find a Mate. The young male contestant explains to the first female that strip poker is his favourite game and asks her: 'Will you go all the way when I let you play with me?' He asks the second young woman: 'Will you let me touch you up, or should I use a stripper?' His question to the third woman is even more direct: 'Will you have sex with me?' The prize is a dirty weekend in Paris, staying at Bonking Motel. It is shocking that a Christian organisation thinks it is necessary to use this type of language to deliver a message to young people. Surely it must know that the Bible warns against obscenity, foolish talk and coarse joking? *(Ephesians 5.4.)*

The video uses a speaking head from the salacious teenage magazine *Just 17* to get its message across. Annabel G of *Just 17* tells teenagers: 'I think saying no if you don't *want* sex is the most crucial word and I don't think it is used often enough' *[my italics]*. A health promotion expert advises: 'There's no need to be apologetic, everybody has got the right to say I don't *want* to have sex with you *now*, and I think young people need to have the confidence to say that, and I think young people need to feel good about saying it, because it can be a very positive choice for young people' *[my italics]*. In other words, young people are being advised that their decision to have sex or not to have sex depends on what they want at that moment in time, and not on any objective standard of right and wrong.

'Parents First'

In 1995 CARE produced a training package *Parents First – Sex Education within the Home*, which encourages parents to talk to their children about sex. It is of such importance that CARE is encouraging all church leaders to consider incorporating *Parents First* into their church teaching programme. CARE warns that while 'the material is firmly based on Christian teaching', the course leader 'may encounter embarrassment, even hostility at first and this needs to be anticipated and worked through'.[4] According to CARE, ground rules for the teaching session should include respect, non-judgementalism, openness, trust and confidentiality.

CARE claims that discussions around sexual language are very important. An activity sheet is handed out which requires parents to categorise a list of sexual words into polite, neutral, clinical and rude/offensive. For example, the words for sex are, sleep with; making love; sexual intercourse and screwing. Other words on the activity sheet are penis, female genitalia, and oral sex. It is stressed that the parents will not have to show their completed activity sheet to anyone else or share their words with the group. If the 'group is quite comfortable with sexual language, the words can be anonymously collated onto a flip chart and used to illustrate the discussion on appropriate sexual language'.[5]

Apparently CARE feels that it is 'important' for Christians to have a vocabulary of lewd words, but why does this information need to be collated anonymously? Is it because the offensive words that it is intended to generate might arouse a sense of shame?

Another activity uses the technique of the values continuum to help 'parents clarify what they actually believe and value about sex and sexuality'. The purpose is to help 'parents realise that within the Christian church there may be a range of beliefs and values held about particular issues'.[6] A pair of value statements is placed at the opposite ends of the room with a clear space between them. For example, 'homosexuality is part of God's created order' is placed at one end of the room and 'homosexuality is against God's created order' at the other end. Parents are then invited to read the statements and decide where they stand on the continuum between these two alternatives. The purpose is to help Christians clarify what they believe. After each pair of statements there must be some discussion. The objective is 'not necessarily to get to a definitive RIGHT answer, but to help parents realise they do hold certain beliefs that they will transmit to their youngsters and that all issues are not easily resolved.'[7] The underlying aim of this technique is to demonstrate that there are no absolute, right answers to moral questions, that there is no absolute moral truth. Parents, therefore, must clarify their position on a moral continuum – this is usually referred to as relative morality, and is diametrically opposed to the absolute moral truth taught in the Bible.

CARE and condoms

We have already seen that a number of CARE counselling centres provide advice on contraception and the morning-after pill. So what does CARE teach about condoms? In its response to the Teenage Parenthood report of the Government's social exclusion unit, CARE makes it clear that, in its view, there is a role for contraceptive centres which offer contraception to young people faced with the possibility of an unplanned pregnancy. 'When a young person visits a centre, communication and discussion with parents, either directly or by encouraging the girl to speak to her parents, is seen as an important part of supporting the girl as she considers the options open to her. In addition, young people's advice centres and specifically dedicated family planning facilities can be effective especially if young people are given an opportunity to discuss their situation and decision-making as well as being provided with contraception, if appropriate.'[8] CARE believes 'that it is not appropriate to make contraception available to young people in the absence of discussion and advice, so casual distribution of condoms for example at youth clubs or schools is not acceptable.'[9] However, CARE registers no objection to contraceptive clinics for young people, which provide advice on how to use contraception, such as those run by Brook and the NHS.

CARE's new *Evaluate . . . informing choice* sex education programme claims to be 'a Sex & Relationship Education programme which, using a set of dynamic, relevant and interactive multimedia presentations, empowers young people to make healthy informed choices, and supports them in delaying sexual experience until a committed relationship, ideally marriage'. The programme is 'delivered by teams of highly trained educators to pupils age 11 and over'.[10] CARE aims to assist 'developing life skills to enable young people to make healthy and well-informed decisions' regarding their sex life. It claims that the content of the sex education presentations will lead to informed decision-making.

The following quotation from CARE's policy document outlines its position on condoms: 'As the *Evaluate* programme provides education about choices available to people in the light of HIV & AIDS and other sexually transmitted infections, this will include education about condom use. The *Evaluate* programme does not promote the exclusive use of condoms as the only choice for young people with regard to sexual behaviour. Rather, *Evaluate* educators provide such education in accordance with the World Health Organisation position, which is "abstinence and fidelity between uninfected partners and safer sex can prevent the transmission of HIV. Safer sex includes non-penetrative sex and sex using condoms." *Evaluate* educators do not give out condoms in schools nor are condom demonstrators part of these demonstrations.' So we see that CARE's version of 'safer sex' includes teaching children about both condoms and non-penetrative sex. The reason for teaching non-penetrative sex is to show children how they can achieve sexual gratification without resorting to vaginal sex. The underlying aim is to encourage school pupils to think about stages of sexual intimacy, which include oral sex, anal sex, and mutual masturbation, as alternatives to sexual intercourse. The theory behind this programme is that if children can be taught the pleasures of non-penetrative sex they will be less likely to indulge in vaginal sex, thereby reducing the rates of teenage pregnancy.

A World Health Organisation (WHO) position statement on *Condoms and HIV Prevention* (July 2004) asserts that 'condoms are an integral and essential part of comprehensive prevention and care programmes, and their promotion must be accelerated . . . Condoms are a key component of combination prevention strategies individuals can choose at different times in their lives to reduce their risks of sexual exposure to HIV. These include delay of sexual initiation, abstinence, being safer by being faithful to one's partner when both partners are uninfected and consistently faithful, reducing the number of sexual partners, and correct and consistent use of condoms.'

So we see that CARE's message to children about condoms is based not on Scripture, but on the advice of the World Health Organisation. And the WHO position is fully supported by the International Planned Parenthood Federation (IPPF). In October 1999 the WHO met with a number of organisations, including the IPPF to produce a joint policy statement on dual protection against unwanted pregnancies and sexually transmitted infections, including HIV. The statement claimed that: 'Informed choice must also include the acknowledgement that the condom, when used correctly and consistently, not only prevents HIV and STIs, but can also be a highly effective contraceptive.' So CARE's bedfellows in teaching about condoms are the WHO and the IPPF.

CARE's approach similar to the FPA and Brook

My book on sex education, *Lessons in Depravity*, documents the link between the sexual revolutionaries, such as Marie Stopes, Sigmund Freud and Alfred Kinsey, and sex education. A chapter is devoted to the so-called 'Christian' version of sex education. Having spent many hours studying various documents and reports, I reached the conclusion that CARE's approach to sex education is characterised by moral relativism – in CARE's version of sex education there are no moral absolutes. No form of sexual activity is ever condemned as wrong.

In *Lessons in Depravity* I comment: 'So we must ask the question: In what way does CARE's version of sex education differ from that of the sexual revolutionaries? CARE, like the FPA and Brook, believes that children should be taught about sex in primary school, starting at the age of five. CARE, like the FPA and Brook, believes that primary schoolchildren should be taught a sexual vocabulary. CARE, like the FPA and Brook, believes that parents should be encouraged to talk to their children about sex. CARE, like the FPA and Brook, believes that children should be taught the facts about sexual intercourse, STDs, abortion and contraception. CARE, like the FPA and Brook, believes that dedicated family planning clinics which give young people advice on how to use contraception, can be effective. CARE, like Brook and the FPA, has used the teenage magazine *Just 17* to promote its sex education messages. CARE, like the FPA and Brook, promotes moral relativism.'[11]

So CARE's approach to abortion and sex education are both grounded in moral relativism. Therefore, whatever they say to the contrary, CARE's non-directive, non-judgemental ideology makes void the absolutes of God's moral law. Slowly but surely CARE has deserted the way of truth and is now comfortable in its postmodern worldview. The tragedy is that it claims to speak in the name of the Christian church.

Characteristics of false teachers

Many people will find it difficult to believe that an organisation of CARE's standing has introduced false teaching into the church. *Lessons in Depravity* was criticised because it was seen to be attacking the work of Christian organisations with the same apparent ease that it attacked secular organisations such as Brook and the FPA.[12] The sentiment was that I was wrong to challenge the teaching of those who claim to be Christian, although no attempt was made to address the substance of the criticism. But this is not the way of the Bible. True Christian unity is founded in truth; false teaching must be exposed for what it is. The apostle Peter warns that just as there were false prophets among the people of God, there will be false teachers in the church who 'will secretly bring in destructive heresies' *(2 Peter 2.1)*.

God's prophet Jeremiah opposed the false prophets who followed an evil course and misled the people of God. The prophet declared the words of the Lord: 'Both prophet and priest are profane; yes, in My house I have found their wickedness . . . They speak a vision of their own heart, not from the mouth of the Lord . . . I have not sent these prophets, yet they ran. I have not spoken to them, yet they prophesied. But if they had stood in My counsel, and had caused My people to hear My words, then they would have turned them from their evil way and from the evil of their doings' *(Jeremiah 23.11, 16, 21-22)*.

Here the Scriptures draw a sharp distinction between those who have stood in the counsel of the Lord and the false teachers. The characteristic of those who have stood in the counsel of the Lord is that they proclaim the word of the Lord. And the one who has the word of the Lord must speak it faithfully, while the people, when they hear the word of the Lord, turn from their evil ways and from their evil deeds. '"Is not My word like a fire?" says the Lord, "and like a hammer that breaks the rock in pieces?"' *(Jeremiah 23.29.)*

The false teachers, on the other hand, speak the visions and delusions of their own minds, not the word of the Lord. '"Therefore behold, I am against the prophets," says the Lord, "who steal My words every one from his neighbour. Behold, I am against the prophets," says the Lord, "who use their tongues and say, 'He says.' Behold, I am against those who prophesy false dreams," says the Lord, "and tell them, and cause My people to err by their lies and by their recklessness. Yet I did not send them or command them; therefore they shall not profit this people at all," says the Lord' *(Jeremiah 23.30-32)*. They steal words from one another, as CARE has taken the words of secular psychology and the WHO, and proclaimed them to be consistent with the word of the Lord. 'They continually say to those who despise Me, "The Lord has said, 'You shall have peace'"; and to everyone who walks according to the imagination of his own heart, "No evil shall come upon you"' *(Jeremiah 23.17)*. That is, the false prophets provide those who rebel against the word of the Lord with a false sense of security. The false teacher is the one who promises the woman who is considering abortion that she can go ahead because God is always willing to forgive. They strengthen the hands of evildoers so that no one turns from wickedness.

In view of the biblical teaching on false prophets it is not difficult to see that CARE's non-directive, option counselling is not from the counsel of the Lord. CARE is not faithfully proclaiming the word of the Lord, but the delusions and visions of its own mind.

CARE's false teaching

CARE's pro-choice ideology is anathema to the Christian faith. CARE has succeeded in de-moralising the issue of abortion. To promise to a pregnant woman that its counsellors will 'help you find out what you want to do'[13] with the life of her unborn baby is consistent with the pagan creed 'do what you will, as long as it harms none'. Another characteristic of paganism is that it rejects God's moral law, which it pejoratively refers to as a list of thou-shalt-nots.[14] It does not take much insight to see that CARE's pro-choice ideology, which encourages a woman to do as she *wants* with her pregnancy, is perfectly consistent with the pagan ethic. By offering a pregnant woman the option of abortion CARE has legitimised lawlessness. By giving a pregnant woman non-directive advice regarding her pregnancy, CARE is following the doctrine of moral relativism. By persuading a woman that her feelings are a guide to what she should do about her pregnancy, CARE is rejecting the word of the Lord. Taken as a whole, CARE's ideology is based in amoral postmodernism and CARE is an apostate organisation.

The evidence examined in this book suggests that CARE, by presenting its options counselling under the auspices of the church, and by promising certain forgiveness for those who abort their children, is actually encouraging women to accept abortion. While they no doubt care for the life of the unborn child, they behave as though they do not. Therefore they are not a voice for the voiceless, but a voice for the pro-abortion movement. How did they move into this position? The Bible warns of the false teachers who have 'crept in unnoticed . . . ungodly men, who turn the grace of our God into licentiousness and deny the only Lord God and our Lord Jesus Christ' *(Jude 4)*. And, 'Now as Jannes and Jambres resisted Moses, so do these also resist the truth: men of corrupt minds, disapproved concerning the faith; but they will progress no further, for their folly will be manifest to all, as theirs also was' *(2 Timothy 3.8, 9)*.

This is an extremely important issue for evangelical churches in the UK, for CARE is an organisation that has been born and nurtured in the cradle of evangelical Christianity. For over a decade CARE's false teaching has flourished within the bosom of evangelical Christianity. With open arms many evangelical churches, some perhaps noting the *claims* of CARE rather than the *methods*, have welcomed CARE's pro-choice dogma, and scores of pregnancy counselling centres have grown up around evangelical churches. With open wallets evangelicals have supported CARE's ministry. In the case of many churches, however, they have become so weak in recognising moral compromise, that they have proved unable to distinguish between pro-choice counselling and biblical truth.

The God of the Bible hates evil and in *Deuteronomy* commands His people six times to purge the evil from among them. Sin in the midst of God's people arouses the wrath of God and weakens the witness of the church. We have the example of Achan's sin described in *Joshua 7*. God commanded the people to keep away from the accursed things in Jericho. 'By all means keep yourselves from the accursed things, lest you become accursed when you take of the accursed things, and make the camp of Israel a curse, and trouble it' *(Joshua 6.18)*. But Achan wilfully disobeyed God's command and took some of those things and hid them in the ground in his tent. He had violated the covenant of the Lord and done a disgraceful thing in Israel *(Joshua 7.15)*. 'So the anger of the Lord burned against the children of Israel' because of Achan's sin, and they were defeated by their enemy *(Joshua 7.1)*. The Lord warned Israel: 'Neither will I be with you anymore, unless you destroy the accursed from among you' (v 12). Dale Ralph Davis comments on the implication of Achan's sin for the church: 'Would it be going too far to say that the apparent absence of God in various segments of the church may be due to our unwillingness to purge evil from our midst by the costly exercise of church discipline? . . . Our problem is that we prefer the tolerance of men to the praise of God.'

The Lord's holiness 'demands that He stand opposed to evil and sin just as light stands opposed to darkness. The two are incompatible. And because this holiness, this light, is divine goodness, His opposition is not the passive resistance of a mere spectator. His holiness rises up in active resistance to all evil, to all that cheapens and distorts and destroys His creatures. The Holy One, in His perfect goodness, is actively and intensely set against evil. He judges it as the only holy Judge of all His creatures.'[15] There can be no compromise with the detestable teachings of pro-choice options counselling. God's people cannot flourish if they harbour this evil in their midst. CARE's pro-choice counselling is an issue that evangelicals cannot duck or fudge. Leaders of evangelical witness in the UK must consider their relationship to CARE. It is not good enough to say that Christians must not attack each other. False teaching has no place in the church of Christ.

The fact that CARE's pro-choice abortion counselling has flourished in evangelical circles is clear evidence of the lack of concern over mass abortion that disfigures the face of Great Britain. Evangelicals have been more than happy to leave the issue in the hands of CARE. And so the whole land is being polluted with the blood of the innocents because there is no one who cares. The Lord warns that 'the whole land is made desolate, because no one takes it to heart' *(Jeremiah 12.11)*.

Endnotes

1 CARE website, Caring, Pregnancy/Post-abortion, Making a decision.

2 Hull Crisis Pregnancy Centre website.

3 CARE, 2003 Annual Report, pp 4-5.

4 *Parents First – Sex Education within the Home*, CARE, 1995, p 5.

5 Ibid. p 35.

6 Ibid. p 46.

7 Ibid. p 48.

8 *Teenage* parenthood, A submission to the Social Exclusion Unit, CARE, November 1998, p 15-16.

9 Ibid. p 16.

10 CARE, The document, Education Policy, Aims & Code of Conduct.

11 E. S. Williams, *Lessons in Depravity*, Belmont House Publishing, London, 2003, p 290.

12 *Evangelicals Now*, March 2004, Book Review, *Lessons in Depravity*, Dr Trevor Stammers.

13 CARE Centres Network website, It's positive – what are my options?

14 The Pagan Federation website, paganfed.demon.co.uk.

15 Thomas Trevethan, *The Beauty of God's Holiness*, InterVarsity Press, 1995, p 101.

6

Christian Teaching about Abortion

THE BIBLE makes it clear we live in a moral universe. All human beings, whether they recognise it or not, are subject to the moral law of God. And all who are under the law will be judged by the law. God has put His laws into the human heart and so we have a conscience that warns us against wrongdoing. Most women know that abortion is wrong, and suffer guilt as a consequence. Christians have a duty to warn those contemplating abortion of the consequences of their actions. The Bible is clear that God's people cannot stand back in the face of mass abortion that is now part of the culture of this nation.

We must witness against the evil of abortion. We are to do all that we can within the law to save the life of the unborn. The Lord has commissioned His people very clearly – 'Deliver those who are drawn toward death, and hold back those stumbling to the slaughter. If you say, "Surely we did not know this," Does not He who weighs the hearts consider it? He who keeps your soul, does He not know it? And will He not render to each man according to his deeds?' *(Proverbs 24.11-12.)*

1. The value of human life

The Christian church believes that human life created in the image of God is of overwhelming value. The life of every human, in God's eyes, is precious. Numerous scriptures point to the personhood of the unborn child. King David, for example, acknowledges God's creative purposes in the womb. 'For You have formed my inward parts; You have covered me in my mother's womb . . . Your eyes saw my substance, being yet unformed' *(Psalm 139.13, 16)*. The word of the Lord came to Jeremiah: 'Before I formed you in the womb I knew you; before you were born I sanctified you; and I ordained you a prophet to the nations' *(Jeremiah 1.5)*. Job, in his plea to God declares: 'Your hands have made me and fashioned me . . . Remember, I pray, that You have made me like clay . . . Did You not . . . clothe me with skin and flesh, and knit me together with bones and sinews? You have granted me life and favour, and Your care has preserved my spirit' *(Job 10.8-9, 11-12)*. Job acknowledges that God's steadfast love, which he had known throughout his life, started in the womb when God's hands fashioned and made him into a human being.

The incarnation of Christ bears witness to the personhood of the unborn. The angel Gabriel explains the purposes of God to Mary. 'And behold, you will conceive in your womb and bring forth a Son, and shall call His name Jesus . . . The Holy Spirit will come upon you, and the power of the Highest will overshadow you; therefore, also, that Holy One who is to be born will be called the Son of God' *(Luke 1.31, 35)*. The Scriptures recognise Jesus as the Messiah from the time of His conception. When Mary greets Elizabeth, the babe John leaps for joy in her womb *(Luke 1.44)*. The unborn prophet, John the Baptist, recognises the unborn Messiah. This remarkable Bible story describes the relationship between two as yet unborn children, thereby illustrating God's view of the unborn child. Both are named by God while still in their mother's womb, and both have a place in God's plan of salvation while still in the womb.

The Greek word *brephos* is used to describe the unborn John. The word *brephos*, as used in the Scriptures, describes the unborn, the new-born and the infant *(1 Peter 2.2, Acts 7.19, Luke 18.15)*. Indeed, the Scriptures make no differentiation between the unborn child and the newborn child, and neither should we.

The pro-choice movement denies the personhood of the unborn child. The unborn child is routinely referred to as a foetus, with the implication that the foetus is something less than a person. Because pro-choice dogma regards the life of the unborn as dispensable, abortion can be presented as an option. The counselling provided by CARE, analysed above, makes no attempt to explain the biblical view of the unborn child, and no attempt to protect the life of the unborn child. According to *Making a Decision*, the unborn baby is simply one item to consider along with a number of others as a woman writes a list of her losses and gains to help her decide whether or not abortion is the best thing for her.

2. Abortion is murder

The purpose of the sixth commandment, 'You shall not murder' *(Exodus 20.13)*, is to protect human life. According to the Bible, murder is the intentional killing of innocent human life. The murder scenarios described in *Numbers 35* all illustrate an intention to kill. For example, 'If he strikes him with an iron implement *[for example, a curette]*, so that he dies, he is a murderer; the murderer shall surely be put to death . . . If he pushes him out of hatred or, while lying in wait, hurls something at him so that he dies, or in enmity he strikes him with his hand so that he dies . . . he is a murderer' *(Numbers 35.16, 20, 21)*. To purposely destroy a human being, with malice aforethought, is murder. To purposely destroy an unborn child in its mother's womb, with malice aforethought, is intentional killing, and that, according to Scripture, is murder.

John Calvin believed that abortion was murder. He wrote in his commentary on *Exodus 21*: '. . . for the foetus, though enclosed in the womb of its mother, is already a human being, and it is a monstrous crime to rob it of the life which it has not yet begun to enjoy. If it seems more horrible to kill a man in his own house than in a field, because a man's house is his place of most secure refuge, it ought surely to be deemed more atrocious to destroy a foetus in the womb before it has come to light.'[1]

The shocking reality is that around 180,000 unborn children are being murdered in the UK each year. The shocking reality is that CARE's counselling, in the name of the Christian church, offers a pregnant woman the option of murdering her unborn child.

3. The shedding of innocent blood

Child sacrifice was common practice among the Canaanites. Children were sacrificed to the god Molech, a practice that was an abomination in the eyes of God. The God of the Bible hates hands that shed innocent blood (*Proverbs 6.17*). And God warns His people that innocent blood must not be shed in their land. 'You shall put away the guilt of innocent blood from Israel, that it may go well with you' *(Deuteronomy 19.13)*. Yet the unthinkable occurred. When Israel became involved in idol worship, 'They even sacrificed their sons and their daughters to demons, and shed innocent blood, even the blood of their sons and daughters, whom they sacrificed to the idols of Canaan; and the land was polluted with blood' *(Psalm 106.37, 38)*. On the high places of Baal children were sacrificed, and the valley of Hinnom became the Valley of Slaughter *(Jeremiah 7.32)*. The killing of the innocents was the sign of a godless society given over to evil. Such a society was a stench in the nostrils of God. Because human beings are created in the image of God, the shedding of innocent blood cries out to God for judgement. 'So you shall not pollute the land where you are; for blood defiles the land, and no atonement can be made for the land, for the blood that is shed on it, except by the blood of him who shed it' *(Numbers 35.33)*.

Today, modern Britain has become the Valley of Slaughter as around

700 babies are killed each weekday. The UK flows with the blood of unborn children. The UK has been polluted with the blood of the innocents, and their blood cries out to God for vengeance.

4. The counsel of the Lord

The prophet Jeremiah records the rebellion of Israel against the law of God. The land was full of adulterers, yet the religious leaders (priests) were living a lie and strengthening the hands of evildoers, so that no one turned from his evil. They spoke visions from their own minds, saying, 'No harm will come to you.' Today CARE is expressing the same attitude to abortion. Women are offered the freedom to choose without pressure, condemnation or judgement. The most important thing is that a woman makes an informed choice she can live with. But if they had stood in the counsel of the Lord, then they would have proclaimed God's words to His people, and 'they would have turned them from their evil way and from the evil of their doings' (Jeremiah 23.22). One of the reasons for the feeble response of the Christian church to the abortion holocaust is that many Christian leaders are not standing in the counsel of the Lord. Many churches are deeply compromised by their association with CARE. Many are speaking their own words, using their own reasonable arguments, expressing their own ideas, instead of speaking the word of the Lord.

5. The deception of abortion

One of the reasons why abortion has become acceptable in our society is that the pro-abortion lobby has been remarkably successful in disguising the true nature of abortion. Because abortion is done in secret, behind the walls of an abortion clinic, there is no understanding in society of the real nature of abortion. The blood of the unborn is crying out for the truth to be told. As Christians we must witness to the reality of abortion. We should always refer to the unborn child as an unborn child; we should always refer to abortion as killing, and we should remind society that abortion, in God's eyes, is murder of the innocent unborn. We should explain that abortion is not a termination of a pregnancy but the killing of an unborn child. We must warn of the inevitable guilt and sadness that follows abortion.

6. The true Christian response

Abortion is the greatest moral evil of our time. The true Christian response is to oppose abortion, and to warn of its consequences. True Christian compassion is to witness to the evil of abortion. Christians should come alongside women with unwanted pregnancies and explain the promises and warnings contained in God's Word. Many will be open to the Gospel of salvation, and most will be grateful for clear biblical guidance on why abortion is not an option. Women who are considering abortion should be warned of the inevitable moral and spiritual consequences. Everything possible should be done to persuade them of the folly of abortion. Everything possible should be done to save the life of the unborn child. Those women who choose to follow the broad way of abortion must be warned that it leads to destruction.

According to Francis Schaeffer, 'Of all the subjects relating to the erosion of the sanctity of human life, abortion is the keystone. It is the first and crucial issue that has been overwhelming in changing attitudes toward the value of life in general.'[2] In *Whatever Happened to the Human Race?* he writes: 'If, in this last part of the twentieth century, the Christian community does not take a prolonged and vocal stand for the dignity of the individual, for each person's right to life – for the right of each individual to be treated as created in the image of God, rather than as a collection of molecules with no unique value – we feel that as Christians we have failed the greatest moral test to be put before us in this century.

'Future generations will look back, and many will either scoff or believe in Christ on the basis of whether we Christians of today took a sacrificial stand in our various walks of life on these overwhelmingly important issues. If we do not take a stand here and now, we certainly cannot lay any claim to being the salt of the earth in our generation.

We are neither preserving moral values and the dignity of the individual nor showing compassion for our fellow human beings.'[3]

Those who would oppose abortion must understand that they are involved in a spiritual battle against the powers of evil in high places *(Ephesians 6.12)*. The battle is the Lord's. King David understood this truth when he defeated the mighty Goliath, a giant who defied the armies of the living God, with a sling and faith in God *(1 Samuel 17)*. The weapon with which to slay the abortion giant is the sword of the Spirit, which is the Word of God *(Ephesians 6.17)*.

Endnotes

1 John Calvin, *Commentaries on the Last Four Books of Moses*, translated Charles Bingham, Grand Rapids, Eerdmans, 1950, 3: p 42.
2 Francis Schaeffer and Everett Koop, *Whatever Happened to the Human Race?*, Marshall Morgan & Scott, 1980, p 19.
3 Ibid. p 156.

WHAT IS GOING ON IN
CHRISTIAN CRISIS PREGNANCY
COUNSELLING?

This title may be obtained from all Christian
bookshops, or from Amazon

Also available from:

Tabernacle Bookshop
Metropolitan Tabernacle
Elephant & Castle
London SE1 6SD

Tel: 020 7735 7076
Email: Bookshop@MetropolitanTabernacle.org
www.TabernacleBookshop.org